MW00526468

"In *A Kind of Solitude*, Jamie H‹ iar but beautiful healing path of his own agitated way of the Cross. Are you as done as I am with the rah-rah 'gospel' of triumphalist platitudes and ready for some real and raw good news? Jamie is a man who's limped through the sorrow of Gethsemane, known the dying gasps of Golgotha, and beheld the Easter sunrise of resurrection life. Follow him on this tender retreat and I'm sure, like me, you'll breathe your own sighs of solace and hope."

—BRADLEY JERSAK
Dean of Theology & Culture, St. Stephen's University,
New Brunswick

"In this story of a man with a broken heart and the healing power of an icon, Jamie Howison recounts how, with the aid of ancient spiritual insights and practices, and the faithfulness of an undergraduate Christian community in Halifax, a remarkable transformation took place in his life. St. Augustine said that the soul is like a 'waterless land,' and in this journal we see the divine gardener at work, bringing about restoration and new life. This testimony will bring hope to others who long to see God while in a place of disillusionment and desperation."

—STEPHEN ANDREWS
Principal, Wycliffe College, Toronto

"*A Kind of Solitude* is a must-read for pastors and anyone who is interested in the spiritual life. It is a story of death and resurrection, from darkness to light. There are very few brutally honest spiritual memoirs, and this one of them. Life is difficult, and often, downright impossible, and Jamie's story shows us how we can transform our pain into something beautiful."

—WILLIAM C. MILLS
Eastern Orthodox priest and author of
Losing My Religion: A Memoir of Faith and Finding

"This brief memoir of a time set apart for spiritual and emotional healing is a loving appreciation of the abiding power of the church's ancient spiritual traditions to sustain and nourish our souls—and of the hospitality of a community which seeks to be formed by that tradition, so as to be able to 'bear one another's burdens,' as Christ has done for us all."

—LISA WANG
Adjunct Faculty, Trinity College Faculty of Divinity, Toronto

"Jamie Howison writes reverently, personally, and beautifully about the restoration of his own shattered soul after having submitted to the care of a wise spiritual director who knows and trusts the medicinal qualities of ancient spiritual practices and traditions. If you are inclined to suspect there may be medicinal properties to such practices, this book should convince you once and for all."

—STEVE BELL
Recording artist and author

"The book's central insight comes through the author's personal tussle with the wisdom of Abba John the Little, who observed how 'we have abandoned a light burden, namely self-criticism, and taken up a heavy burden, namely self-justification.' Simple to say; hard to live. This story reveals glimmers of providence in the darkness of despair, a testament to the possibility of healing and renewal for all who earnestly seek it."

—DOUG KOOP
Hospital Spiritual Health Practitioner
and former editor of *ChristianWeek*

A Kind of Solitude

April 2021

To Samantha + Anass,
with respect + affection,

Under the mercy,

[signature]

A Kind of Solitude

How Pacing the Cage with an Icon
and *The Book of Common Prayer*
Restored My Soul

Jamie Howison

RESOURCE *Publications* • Eugene, Oregon

A KIND OF SOLITUDE
How Pacing the Cage with an Icon and *The Book of Common Prayer* Restored My Soul

Resource Publications
An Imprint of Wipf and Stock Publishers
199 W. 8th Ave., Suite 3
Eugene, OR 97401

www.wipfandstock.com

PAPERBACK ISBN: 978-1-7252-9278-9
HARDCOVER ISBN: 978-1-7252-9279-6
EBOOK ISBN: 978-1-7252-9280-2

02/19/21

This book is dedicated with gratitude to the community of
King's College Chapel, with special thanks to
Father Gary Thorne and Ben von Bredow.

Contents

Preface

THE STORY TOLD AND reflections shared in this book have as their background a deep personal crisis. In July 2016, my marriage of eighteen years came to an abrupt end, something I had not seen coming. I'm not going to go into the details of that story, because it is not mine alone to tell.

Madeleine L'Engle characterized her own marriage as a "two-part invention,"[1] and I suppose it is equally true that the dissolution of a marriage is at some level not unlike that, a narrative with more than one part. I've come to realize that in my case there are at least three stories at work: the shared story that speaks to how we began, how we grew, and all of the ups and downs we went through together—and then two more, sometimes very distinct and even conflicting stories, about what for each of us was right, and what was wrong, in it all.

In good conscience I really can't write about those stories. But I can write about my own restoration, and specifically about the five weeks I spent living in a kind of solitude in the context of the Chapel community of the University of King's College in Halifax, Nova Scotia.

I offer these words with deep gratitude and humility. I am profoundly thankful for the kind of support I received from friends, family, and my church over the six months prior to my departure for Halifax, and I do not take for granted the gift of being able to step away from my church community for those five weeks.

1. L'Engle, *Two-Part Invention*.

I am well aware that most people facing such a crisis do not have the luxury of that sort of time, or the opportunity to be immersed in the disciplines that were offered me at King's.

A key character in this narrative is Father Gary Thorne, who was at the time Chaplain of the King's College Chapel. He is a colleague and mentor, and above all else a treasured and valued friend. In my opening and closing chapters here, I refer to him simply as Gary, because that is how I've known him for years. However, in the chapters that walk through my five weeks in Halifax, I refer to him as "Father Thorne," in part because that is how he was addressed by the Chapel community, but more importantly because during those weeks I placed myself firmly under his guidance and authority, making the more formal and traditionally catholic manner of address the right one.

Thanks are due to my church community of saint benedict's table in Winnipeg for making it possible for me to take that time away, and especially to our little staff team from that winter—Rachel Twigg, Kalyn Falk, Larry Campbell, and Carolyn Mount—for going the extra mile. Thanks to the circle of friends who received my occasional email updates, and who held me in prayer over those weeks. To my family, both north and south of the 49th parallel, who trusted that in time all would be well, and who were willing and able to say as much. To David Widdicombe, Kirsten Pinto Gfroerer, Ranall Ingalls, and William Mills, for the different ways you spoke the right words at precisely the right moments. To my sister, Patricia Robertson, for her careful copy-editing and wise counsel. My deepest thanks go to the King's College Chapel community, and especially to Father Gary Thorne and Ben von Bredow. I could not have asked for better guides.

I give thanks to God, that I was invited to taste the very thing of which the Psalmist wrote: "heaviness may endure for the night, but joy cometh in the morning."[2]

---

2. Psalm 30:5, *The Book of Common Prayer.*

The Story before the Story Begins

IN THE DAYS IMMEDIATELY following my realization that my marriage was in deep trouble—that at the very least I was facing a separation, and quite probably a permanent dissolution—my emotions swung wildly between anxious fear and desperate hope. I shook constantly, found myself unable to sleep, lost my appetite, and had trouble keeping down whatever little food I could swallow. I found coffee almost entirely unpalatable, and even the thought of favorite foods like seafood or olives made my stomach lurch. I couldn't focus enough to read or watch a movie, and so late evenings would find me pacing the streets around my home, getting more and more tied up with anxiety, and quite probably compounding my sleeplessness. In my imagination I would conjure up little glimmers of hope, thinking that if I did this or said that or found the right marriage counselor, maybe we could have one more try at things. Faint hope, to be sure—and each time it would fade as quickly as it had come.

Five days in to this I realized that I needed to see my doctor. I wasn't sure what he could offer, and I certainly wasn't looking for medication, but I knew that this was not a sustainable way of living. As it turned out, my doctor could not see me for another ten days, so I opted to go to a nearby community health clinic which listed "stress or anxiety" as one of the health issues for which services were offered. I was ushered into an examination room, and was seen by a nurse practitioner. When she asked what had brought me to the clinic, I broke down in tears and haltingly began to recount all that had happened over those past five days. She listened, jotted down notes in the file, and asked questions about my physical symptoms. When that was done she put down her pen, pushed back from the desk, and fixed her eyes on mine. Everything to this point felt very professional, perhaps even dispassionate, but the eye contact signaled a change. She said, "Everything you are feeling is a completely normal reaction to what is happening in your life. You should still keep your appointment with your doctor, but I don't believe you need medication for anxiety or depression at this stage. You do need to try to sleep, but more than anything you need to talk and talk and talk some more. Do you have family and friends you can trust?"

"Yes, I do, very much so." A very close friend had spent two long evenings with me, and I was seeing another good friend later that afternoon. I had my adult daughters and my mother, too, and I knew they would be there for me.

"You need to keep talking to them, and to find other friends who will be with you through those long evenings. You might also see a counselor, but good friends will be the ones who will see you through, especially over those hard evenings."

"Yes, yes, I know that. I really do."

As I stood to go, she again looked me directly in the eye. "Keep your appointment with your doctor, and if things are getting worse you can come back here or go to Emergency. Just keep talking to your friends."

And I did. For the better part of two months I made sure I had someone with me on any evening I was going to be home on my own.

When I did see my doctor, he echoed what the nurse practitioner had said, though he was even more concerned about my sleep. "I don't believe you need any sort antidepressant," he said. "This is all a normal reaction to what you've experienced, and I'm not convinced that a medication for depression or anxiety would in the end be helpful." I think that, without quite saying it, he was trying to tell me that the only way through the hard days was just to go through them, to let time and talk do their own kind of work. I appreciated that, even in that moment. "But," he continued, "we do have to get your sleep patterns back in order. I'm going to prescribe a mild sleeping medication that I want you to take about an hour before going to bed. It should give you four or five uninterrupted hours of sleep, which will be a good start." And so for the first time in my life I was taking sleeping meds, which, I am thankful, did exactly what he had said they would. Mornings still came very, very early, and it was rare that I was in bed much later than 5:30 or 6:00 a.m., but it was a start. Buoyed by the sleep, I found I had a little more emotional strength, and that I was becoming a little less shaky.

One of the people who had been a most important support was my friend David Widdicombe, who had spent those two evenings with me over the first five days of my crisis, and then another long evening during the second week. Both a trusted friend and a valued ministry colleague, he was set to go away on an extended study leave, and so we arranged a final conversation before his departure. It was a Saturday afternoon, and this time rather than coming to my home he thought it would be best to meet for lunch in a quiet restaurant. I suspect he thought it would be good to get me away from the house, and to see that I had something nutritious to eat. He was probably right on both counts. As we sat and talked, he looked at me and said, "Jamie, if you were a layperson, I'd be referring you to a therapist. But you're not. You're a priest, with a deep interior life. What you need is a proper Anglo-Catholic spiritual director—a priest, older than you, someone whose authority you can trust."

"I think you're right," I replied. "But who? There really isn't anyone close by who seems right for that."

"I don't know. Maybe you can ask your connections in Toronto if there is someone there. You could go for a couple of weeks, stay at Holy Cross Priory, and meet with a spiritual director four or five times over the course of your time there."

That seemed a good idea, and I did know someone in Toronto to contact about this. The seed was planted, and as soon as I got home, I fired off an email message to my friend in Toronto to see what she might recommend.

The next day I arrived at the church for our evening liturgy, ready to preach and preside at the Eucharist. Sundays were a bit of a study for me during those months, in that no matter how anxious or emotional I was the rest of the week, the moment I stepped into the church it was as if I were reminded—in my body as well as in my head and heart—who I really was. Not that I didn't still harbor fears about what people might think or feel; would they be disappointed, angry, or simply confused? I am sure that different people did experience such reactions, yet as a whole our church community seemed able to set its reactions aside to accept and support me in all of my hurts and fears. The support was palpable, and standing to preach, or at the table celebrating communion, the ground under my feet felt more solid than any other place I might stand. In the same way, sermon-writing was not a struggle, because it felt familiar. These are things that I knew how to do. No, more than that: this is when I know who I am. Even though on some of those Sundays I felt a low-grade dread all through the day, just walking into the church building for our evening liturgy shifted it away.

On that particular Sunday, the day after my conversation with David about seeking out a spiritual director, I found a letter waiting for me in my mail slot at the church. It was from Father Gary Thorne, the Chaplain at the University of King's College in Halifax and a much loved and trusted friend. Beginning in 2004, we had served together for seven years on a theological commission for the Anglican Church of Canada, and over the course of that time our friendship had grown. In 2013 Gary had invited me to spend a week at King's College, lecturing on my recently-released book on the life and work of John Coltrane,[1] preaching in the College Chapel, and generally connecting with the Chapel community there. He had run into my sister who lives in Halifax, heard the news of what was going on for me, and wrote to assure

---

1. *God's Mind in that Music: Theological Reflections through the Music of John Coltrane.* Eugene, OR: Cascade Books, 2012.

me of his prayers: "Of course in this note I shall not express anything other than my unconditional love for you and offer to carry some of your burden."

And then a little further into the letter came this: "Perhaps in God's Providence we might meet again and talk—there are so few who know how to listen: so few but you would be one of the very few with whom a conversation might be possible." My heart began to pound. Maybe Gary was the spiritual director I needed? As I read further, it became more and more clear to me that he was, and by the time I reached the end of his letter I knew I was going to contact him that night. "Trust that if you ask," he wrote, "I shall do anything I can for you. I shall carry your fear as much as you allow. You are not alone. Under the mercy, Gary."

While his letter had been written on good stationery, in fountain pen, my response that night was an email, and his measured, careful, and loving thoughts were met by my urgent and hastily-composed message. I began by telling him that I had read his letter that evening in the hour before our Sunday liturgy, and that its timing had about it a taste of providence. I explained how on the previous day I had spent a couple of hours with a good friend and colleague, and that he had suggested what I most needed was a proper Anglo-Catholic spiritual director to guide me into a disciplined and searching process of confession, prayer, and Eucharist, a priest whose authority I could readily recognize and trust. I told Gary that I had thought much about this over the previous twenty-four hours, and that I had begun to look at the possibility of spending a few weeks in Toronto.

> And then your letter arrived. Gary, I want you to think and pray on this. Were I to arrange to spend several weeks in Halifax, would you consider offering me that kind of direction? I could stay with my sister and her family, though part of me thinks it might be better to find something closer to a retreat style of space. I think it is important that such a time be very intentional, focused, and marked by a good deal of solitude. Of course, I'm already designing things on behalf of a proposed director who has not yet even prayed on this.

So please do give this your prayers, and let me know. The timing will be important, both from a pragmatic point of view—I have commitments at a couple of points in the fall that would be very hard to break—and in terms of what might be best for my soul.

Under the Mercy, indeed.
Jamie

As I waited to hear back, I began to scan my calendar to see when I could block out some time to go to Halifax. The last two weeks of August could work, as would the second half of September and the first few days of October. I checked flights, convinced that I was ready, maybe a bit desperate to go away. It was a full week later that the reply came from Gary, with an explanation that he had been unable to respond earlier because he'd been in a remote park hiking, where he had been "blessed to be without electronic receptivity." There was no real indication as to what he had decided, but there was a rather clear message that it was too early for me to start thinking about booking flights. "You need family to support you unconditionally right now," he wrote. "You need friends to embrace you and to pour the ointment of healing tenderness on your wounds. You need a congregation to hold you up in love and prayer. I am quite certain you have such family, such friends, and such a congregation." And he was right—not only about family, friends and church, but also about it being far too early. I was still too raw, too anxious, to be able to engage deeply with what Gary had in mind.

The next day a far more detailed email message arrived, this time setting out a proposal for how we might proceed. Gary wrote, "I shall assume you can give five to six weeks." Immediately I realized that my looking at a couple of weeks in August or September was not only too soon, it was clearly too short. He went on to outline a plan that had me living in residence at King's, commenting, "I know that you celebrate God's bounty and enjoy his gifts so freely bestowed upon us, but for these six weeks no alcohol and a rigorous diet that is natural and healthy but no-frills." Monday through Friday I would attend daily Morning and Evening Prayer at the College Chapel, with Compline on Monday and Tuesday evenings, while on

Saturdays I would pray the Offices on my own. I would also receive the Eucharist each weekday at King's, and attend a parish church on Sundays. Directed readings would be provided, and I would be expected to keep a journal. I would visit a small Russian Orthodox Hermitage in rural Nova Scotia to spend time in conversation with one of the monks, and at some point would have four days alone in a remote cabin. Okay, I thought, this is not going to be a case of living in the spare room at my sister's house and having regular visits with Father Thorne. No, this is going to be all in, and at five or six weeks it would definitely have to be January and February.

Yes, yes that sounds good. I trust your judgment, Gary, and so if you think that this is the right sort of approach, then I'll start looking at some dates in the winter. Thank you so much, I'll be in touch.

Truthfully, it seemed very far off, and I wondered if I might also need to do something else a bit sooner. I contacted the Collegeville Institute—a center for writers and for academics on sabbatical, with cottage-style apartments located on the grounds at St. John's Abbey in Minnesota—to see if they might have a space for me sometime over the fall, and as it turned out they did have an apartment open in late October and early November. I quickly booked a twelve-day stay, as over the years the Institute has been for me both a productive writing space and a spiritually restorative place to be. Good. Now there was something to look forward to in the not-too-distant future.

At about the same time one of the active lay leaders from the church came by for a visit, during which she said, "Jamie, you seem to be coping okay day by day and Sunday by Sunday, but are any of the plans for the autumn in place?" No, no, not a thing. From one week to the next I know what I have to do and how to do it, but I just can't imagine even thinking about the plans for the fall. She clearly had a sense that this was the case, and so she pitched an idea. We could create two part-time term positions to help cover the next six or seven months, giving me the space and support that I would need to again find truly firm ground. She would fill one of those eight-hour-a-week positions, while another active lay leader would take the other. In fact, she had a proposal for this second person, as the two of them had worked collaboratively as retreat leaders, were both spiritual directors and theologically educated, and were ready to roll into gear if I needed them. Within a week it was all in place, and plans began to be set for the fall. Not that I suddenly had a fully restored ability to look beyond a week at a time: I vividly remember how at our first team meeting I hit my limit after only an hour. We weren't yet finished, but without even thinking I stood up, looked at them, and said, "That's all I've got, I'm afraid." They agreed that we'd covered the ground we most needed to cover, packed up their notebooks and laptops, and then finished their meeting out on the street in front of my house.

Along with the remarkable support offered by friends, family, and the church community, there were other small graces that summer. The house had a lovely screened back porch that overlooked a landscaped yard filled with perennials, a pond, beautiful old shade trees, and a large patio made with reclaimed brick. That porch had long been my favorite place to read, write, and simply "be," and over those months it became the very safest of spaces. There were three different kinds of lilac in the yard, each of which had a different cycle for blooming, and this meant that there were flowering lilacs from the second week of May right through to late June. One day in the middle of August as I walked through the side yard, I noticed a single purple bloom on one of the lilac bushes. In August? Lilacs don't bloom in August. And as that bloom began to fade, another one appeared, and then a third, and I cherished each one as a little consolation. I'm sure that a botanist would be able to explain why it is that lilac bushes occasionally put out a few blooms in August, but I actually didn't much care. That summer it was a threefold gift, utterly gratuitous in the best sense of that word. Each time I walked that path through the side yard, I offered a prayer of thanks for the small graces.

As the summer turned into fall and our new little staff team put things into motion, the ground began to feel a bit more solid under my feet. I had actually been dreading the prospect of winter coming because I would lose my back-porch space. I'd not really been able to be emotionally comfortable in the living room, and when I shared those fears with some friends they took it upon themselves to help rearrange the furniture and art. My daughter's partner was a visual artist, and he and my daughter arrived one day with a freshly-painted canvas to hang in the dining room. When on the October Thanksgiving weekend I did close down the porch, I found that I could find rest in my newly restored living space.

In late October I set out on the six-hour drive to Collegeville, with a plan to return to a long-delayed writing project exploring the connections between the Psalms and the blues. I certainly knew that I needed to spend a good portion of those twelve days in retreat mode, but for me the Institute had also always been about writing. I settled in, read for a bit, made a light dinner, and then walked up the road to the Abbey Church to join the monastic community for Evening Prayer. Early to bed, I thought, will mean a nice early start for tomorrow's writing—and then I woke the next morning with a head cold and absolutely no capacity to concentrate or write. That cold held solid for the next three days, which were all about sleep, pots of tea, and bits of reading. It was unseasonably warm, which meant my afternoons were spent out on my little patio reading in the sun. Even as my cold lifted, I realized that this was the sort of pace that I most needed, and so aside from a few mornings of writing, the entire twelve days was given over to spiritual and emotional respite. I wrote about it for our church website, and along with a bit of description of the Institute and St. John's Abbey, I included the following:

> I always find it a good thing to break from the usual routines and demands of day-to-day life, and to move into a space in which my entire rhythm can change. This is not so much an opportunity to escape the day-to-day as it is a stepping back in order to see it all from a different vantage point. That's a big part of what a retreat is meant to do, you see; to provide a kind of Sabbath, which rejuvenates and enlivens you to return to the everyday with new insights, new perspectives, and renewed commitments.

And then as I drew the reflection to a close, I offered these words:

A Kind of Solitude

My pattern when I'm here is to join the monks for both Midday Prayer and Evening Prayer. The liturgy at noon is simple and brief: a hymn, three psalms, a reading, and prayers, taking no more than about fifteen minutes. Evening Prayer is longer, with a substantial reading, more psalms—some chanted, some spoken, but in both cases very much prayed—and more space and stillness. That's the thing that really draws me in these liturgies . . . the space and stillness. The pacing of those psalms is slow and deliberate, marked by long pauses between verses, which can catch a new visitor quite off guard. For me, though, as soon as I walk into the church I begin to feel as if I'm breathing more deeply than I normally do. By the time I find my space in the choir stalls set aside for visitors (full disclosure . . . creature of habit that I am, unless somebody has beat me to it I always end up in the same stall . . . *my* stall . . .), the gears have utterly shifted. I look up at the great wall of colored glass that runs across the back of the church, and prayer just happens.

And then the liturgy begins, and my prayer moves from personal to corporate. I pray psalms every day as part of my own practice of Evening Prayer, but in the Abbey Church I'm often quite struck by how a particular psalm or verse will pop out at me, as if I'd never seen it before. That's partly because the community uses a different psalm translation from the one I use, but it also has much to do with that pacing, that chanting, that stillness.

Last night at Evening Prayer we chanted Psalm 49, and one verse definitely popped out. In the liturgical translation I normally use, this is how it goes:

"I will incline my ear to a proverb
and set forth my riddle upon the harp." (49:4)

Now, this is how the liturgical translation used at St John's renders it:

"I will turn my mind to a parable,
with the harp I will solve my problem."[2]

"With the harp I will solve my problem"; that is the line that just jumped out at me. I thought immediately of

---

2. In *Saint John's Abbey Prayer* the Psalm translation used is The Grail (England), copyright 1963, 1986.

all of musicians and songwriters at saint benedict's table, and of all the people connected to our community for whom writing music is a way of solving or resolving or working things through. That kind of songwriting is both a way of prayer and a way of doing theology, of thinking about God or contending with God. I'll never again read that psalm in quite the same way, because for me it now marks a kind of honoring of the gift of the musician.

It is the kind of thing you see when you step back and make space for a retreat. You see and you hear and you pray just a little differently, and then suddenly you see something anew.

It is good to be here. Pray for me over the coming week, that this time and place will continue to do its work in my soul, and that I will return both rested and renewed.

Under the mercy,
Jamie

The coming week that I referred to in the closing line of my web post turned out to be a very good one, with both the time and the place doing good and deep work on my soul. On the drive home I found myself feeling deeply rested and quite profoundly restored, and I actually began to wonder if I really needed to go to Halifax. Twice while I was in Collegeville I had searched for flights, and on my first search I'd discovered an incredibly good seat sale that fit my proposed timelines beautifully. It was set to expire within twenty-four hours, so I'd sent a message to Gary to see if my dates—January 10 to February 14—would be workable for him, and whether he was ready to have me book my flight. No answer. I looked again a few days later, again found reasonably priced flights, and sent another email message. Nothing. And so, driving home I began to think that perhaps things were just too busy at King's and that Gary had too much on his plate. *Maybe this isn't really going to work out, and maybe that's okay. I'm feeling stronger and ready to move forward. I'll be fine.*

Shortly after I arrived home, an email message arrived from Gary, opening with these words:

You have been much in my prayers. I have glanced at some of your notes from your retreat. On the one hand I trust that in the past six months you have built up a strength and resiliency of soul that has prepared you for these weeks in Halifax. On the other hand, I suspect that you are wondering if the Halifax trip is needed at all, given your recovered sense of God and self. Good. I have arranged for you to stay in residence at King's.

He has glanced at some of the notes from my retreat, and suspects that I've been wondering if the Halifax trip is needed at all? Good, he says? Book your flights, in other words. I surrender.

We arranged a time for a telephone conversation later in the week, and in that conversation Gary set things out in much more detail even than before. I was to be present among the King's Chapel community as a "Contemplative Theologian in Residence," whose primary work would be to uphold the community in the practice of contemplative prayer, both in public worship and in my room in the College's residence. He had arranged a room for me in an otherwise vacant area of the residence, which was to serve as what he called my "cell" during my five-week residency. Monday through Friday I was to attend Morning Prayer, Holy Communion, Prayers at Mid-Day, and Evening Prayer, as well as the late evening Compline offered on Mondays and Tuesdays. On Saturdays I would be expected to pray the daily Offices on my own, and while I would preside at communion once a week at one of the smaller Chapel gatherings, I would not be asked to preach. I was to keep a journal, but was not to do any other writing; as Gary rightly observed, it would be too easy for me to "get lost in a writing project." I would be expected to get out for a good, long walk at least once a day, because, along with a healthy diet, fresh air, and exercise were important.

Sundays were to be a different sort of day. I was to spend the day with my sister, brother-in-law, and two nieces. They would pick me up in the morning to go to church, after which I would participate in whatever they happened to have planned for the day, ending with dinner at their home. My sister had also convinced

Gary that it would be important if on the second weekend I could join the family in an overnight trip to Prince Edward Island, where my niece Molly was competing in a regional gymnastics competition. Those family times looked like glimmers of Sabbath respite in the midst of what was sounding like a rather demanding time.

Then, as we came to the end of the conversation, Gary asked, "Jamie, would you want to write an icon?"[3]

"Gary, I will do whatever you think is right for me, but I have to tell you that the only things I can draw are stick people and snowmen."

"Good, then you will write an icon. There is a student here who is an iconographer, and I will have him teach you. I will talk to him about it and have him contact you."

"Okay, whatever you think is best," I replied, all the while thinking how awkward it was going to be when that student discovered the limited talent of his understudy.

A few days later another email arrived from Gary with the detailed plan all set out. I learned that for directed reading I would begin with *St Silouan the Athonite* by Archimandrite Sophrony. Neither the saint's nor the author's name was even slightly familiar to me. Private confession was to be involved in my retreat, and I was to come prepared to make a full confession four days after my arrival. It was confirmed that I would spend several days at the Russian Orthodox Hermitage of the Annunciation in Watford, near New Germany, Nova Scotia, engaged in conversation with the abbot, Schema-Igumen Luc, and that I would attend a King's Chapel community retreat on my fourth weekend there. Gary described the Chapel retreat as "an intense weekend with forty

---

3. In the Orthodox tradition, icons are not said to be painted or drawn, but rather written. The iconographer "writes down the text of a certain aspect of the story of our salvation, using images rather than words." Further, "this emphasis on the word *writing* underscores icons' rootedness in the central 'text' of Christianity, that of the incarnation. Writing an icon allows the iconographer to participate in the incarnation's eternal mystery; he uses matter to represent figures and events from the spiritual dimension. The worshiper, in turn, by 'reading' this text through the activity of prayer, also actively participates in this spiritual activity." Zelensky and Gilbert, *Windows to Heaven*, 24.

students or so—all annoyingly bright," adding that I'd also spend two full days in solitude at the retreat location prior to the arrival of the chapel community, "fasting if possible."

Perhaps the most daunting part was that boredom was actually listed as one of the key elements of my daily routine, right along with journaling, chapel services, and icon writing. "It will be difficult," he wrote, "to find the boredom and inner chaos that can lead to a divine restlessness. Spending unproductive time in your cell is important." What in heaven's name did he mean by divine *restlessness*, and could it possibly be something I wanted to cultivate? Peace, acceptance, and restfulness are what I had tasted so deeply in Collegeville. Didn't I need more of that?

In mid-December a very cheerful email message arrived from Ben von Bredow, the student who was to guide me through the writing of an icon. He somewhat apologetically explained that he himself was quite new to iconography, having taken a week-long workshop that had been offered to the King's Chapel community some ten months earlier—yet the images he sent of two of the icons he had written over the summer struck my untrained eye as being very good. Ben wrote about three levels of preparation, the most important being spiritual. "I don't think," he wrote, "that there is anything particular about the spiritual preparation involved in writing an icon that is different from the 'ordinary' preparation of one's soul to receive the Word of God." My own practice of praying a daily Office incorporates intentional stillness followed by a recollective time of intercessory prayer, and it was encouraging that it seemed to sit well with Ben, particularly given that I was already praying that I would be made ready for my extended retreat.

The second level was intellectual preparation, learning something of the theology of iconography. I'd recently been given a book called *Windows to Heaven* by Elizabeth Zelensky and Lela Gilbert. Subtitled "Introducing Icons to Protestants and Catholics," it seemed an ideal fit. I decided I would also revisit Rowan Williams' *The Dwelling of Light*, a Western theologian's reflections on four different icons of Christ from the Eastern tradition. Never one to shy away from books, I considered that level of preparation as good as done.

The third level was what Ben called "physical," by which he meant the basic skill of drawing. Gary had told him that I was not, by my own admission, artistically inclined, so Ben advised that I spend some time with pencil in hand. "In the weeks leading up to coming to Halifax, I suggest finding some pictures online of icons and tracing them for practice or, better, copying them by hand. If you were to spend a half hour or forty-five minutes twice or three times a week just drawing, even though you won't be pleased with what you produce, that will ultimately be very helpful." Well, I thought, maybe in the weeks after Christmas Day I'll give that a try.

Ben then outlined what the process would look like. I was to write a *Pantocrator*, an icon of Christ as ruler of all. Ben would come by for a half hour every day to give me my instructions, and then I would set to work for two or three hours. He had set up a schedule for the work, building in what he called "buffer days" in case the work got delayed along the way. "I will prepare a design over my Christmas break," he wrote, "which you will copy in the first four days of the project." Okay, I thought, he's set aside the first four days—eight or ten hours—for me to copy his design, which means that he really does acknowledge he'll be working with a beginner. At the same time, I couldn't quite fathom how I could possibly spend that much time drawing.

What had I gotten myself in to?

The First Week

January 11–17, 2017

We have abandoned a light burden, namely self-criticism, and taken up a heavy burden, namely self-justification.

ABBA JOHN THE LITTLE, CITED IN A SERMON BY FATHER RANALL INGALLS, JANUARY 12, 2017

I ARRIVED IN HALIFAX on January 10, and after spending the first night with my sister and her family I moved into my rooms at the University of King's College. As Father Thorne had assured me, I was in an otherwise vacant section of the residence, in a suite that would normally be occupied by a residence don. Calling it a suite was a bit of an exaggeration, for while I did have a sitting area (with little furniture other than a couch and a couple of very tired chairs), a bedroom (including a desk), and my own bathroom, there was no kitchen. Instead I had just a little bar fridge, as well as a microwave oven and kettle my sister had lent me, so in order to do any real cooking I would need to head over to a shared student kitchen in another building. It was not uncomfortable, but "Spartan" might be an accurate descriptor.

Through my sitting room window I could look out on to the quadrangle, with its yard and parking circle bordered on all four sides by various College buildings. Directly across the quad I could see the chapel where I was to spend so many hours. Consecrated in

1930, the King's Chapel reflects a high church tradition, with the pews or stalls facing each other across an open aisle, very much in the pattern of an Oxford or Cambridge college chapel. It is not a large space—seating just over one hundred in the fixed pews, with room for another forty chairs in the ante-chapel located at the back of the nave of the church—yet it holds a sort of understated grandeur. It is a good and solid place in which to pray.

King's College Chapel understands itself to be rooted in the Prayer Book tradition of the Anglican Church, and so always uses the Canadian Book of Common Prayer (BCP). The Canadian prayer book of 1962 stands in a direct line from the 1662 Book of Common Prayer of the Church of England (and the 1559 book that preceded it), and so the English of the liturgical texts is essentially Elizabethan. The Psalter is a slightly revised version of Myles Coverdale's 1535 translation of the Book of Psalms. The BCP was by no means unfamiliar to me, as it was this prayer book that drew me originally to Anglicanism when I was a university student. There is a real elegance to the BCP, in both its language and its simplicity, and while many people in the contemporary church find it to be too penitential, strict or heavy-handed, I've always found that ultimately it speaks to me of grace, mercy, and forgiveness.

The King's Chapel community is committed to observing what are called the daily Offices, the BCP's Morning Prayer and Evening Prayer liturgies as well as a brief set of Prayers at Mid-day. The BCP Offices of Morning and Evening Prayer trace their roots to the sevenfold Offices observed in monastic communities shaped by the sixth-century Rule of St Benedict. They are built around the recitation or singing of psalms and biblical canticles and the reading of significant portions of Scripture set out in one-year lectionary cycle, along with prayers and intercessions. Much is repeated every day, and part of the gift of praying a daily Office is in discovering how many of the words have been committed to memory.

My first day on campus was something of a whirlwind of getting settled, oriented, and introduced to all the people I would see over the next five weeks but not really speak with until closer to the end of my time there. The Feast of the Epiphany was celebrated that evening at the 5:00 p.m. Choral Evensong, followed by a big open reception at the Thornes' home. Their rambling old house was full, with everyone feasting on curry and raising glasses of wine in celebration of the day, yet with so many, many new faces I found myself more than just a bit overwhelmed. At one point Father Thorne called for everyone's attention and said, "If you haven't met him yet, this is Father Howison. He'll be with us for the next five weeks as a contemplative theologian in residence, so if you'd like to talk to him you had better do it tonight. Otherwise you'll have to wait until the middle of February!" Laughter all around, followed by warm greetings and welcoming smiles. Yet within minutes I felt I really needed to leave, not because I wanted to get back to my cell but because I needed to further digest what I was beginning to realize I had gotten myself in to.

That first night in my room at King's, I discovered a simple but important fact—namely that the bed was a good one. I slept deeply that night, having retired before 10:00 p.m. with my alarm set for 5:45 the next morning. I've long had a ritual of beginning my day by walking to a coffee shop to get my first cup of the day, and I'd decided that to follow such a ritual in Halifax would give me a familiar anchor with which to mark each day. I'd located a Starbucks just under a kilometer away, and so that day I made my first dark early-morning trek down Coburg Road. I had no internet connectivity at King's, so those morning visits to Starbucks allowed me to send occasional messages to my mother and daughters back in Winnipeg, as well as to communicate a few longer reflections to a circle of people from the church who were holding me in prayer. I also sent regular updates to a friend who was holding my story with particular support and compassion. I set aside internet surfing and using social media entirely. On the days when I had no need of the internet I left my laptop in my room when I went for my coffee, and carried my book and journal with me. I was generally there about an hour, walking back in plenty of time to make a cup of tea before 8 a.m. Morning Prayer.

Ben arrived at my door after Morning Prayer, carrying with him a large pad of newsprint and a little bin of drawing supplies.

As he took out the drawing he had made for me to copy, I felt immediately overwhelmed, even discouraged. It was much bigger than I'd imagined—about 14 by 20 inches—and beautifully drawn with all kinds of detail. "No, no, Father," Ben said (I was almost always addressed as "Father" by the members of the Chapel community). "Don't look at the whole drawing. Look at the sections." With great care he showed me the faint guidelines set out on the sheet, and then took out a ruler and a compass and demonstrated how his drawing was all composed in sections and circles. "Draw your guidelines, make a circle for the halo, and then start in this bottom corner section. See, there are only a few very easy lines there, and once those are done you can move to the next section. And remember, the eraser is your best friend." Okay, I thought, I'll give it a try.

And so I did. Two and a half hours later, with a stiff neck and a sore right hand, I sat back in my chair and looked at what I had done. Not bad, I thought—and it looks a heck of a lot more like Jesus than it does like a snowman. In my journal I simply noted, "I believe I can do this."

That evening at 5:00 was the weekly University Eucharist, and I discovered that the guest preacher was Father Ranall Ingalls, a friend of mine from undergraduate years. Ranall had left Winnipeg in the mid-1980s to pursue his theological education before settling in New Brunswick as a parish priest. We had seen each other only very occasionally over the years, but ours is one of those unique friendships in which it is possible to pick up a conversation after ten years as if no time at all had passed. Father Thorne thought it would be good if Ranall and I went out for dinner together after the liturgy—my first real inkling that while Father Thorne had provided a very definite pattern for my weeks in Halifax, there would be times when he would have me set it aside—and so Ranall and I settled into a cozy restaurant for a good, warming meal. Of course I wanted to catch up on all that had happened in both our lives, but first I needed to talk more about the very fine sermon he had just preached. In particular, I wanted to tell him how powerfully one portion of the sermon had spoken to me, specifically a quotation from Abba John the Little: "We have abandoned a light burden, namely self-criticism, and taken up a heavy burden, namely self-justification." Self-criticism, it seemed to me, was meant in the sense of being prepared to truthfully name and confess our failings and foibles, which is precisely the direction in which the liturgies of the Book of Common Prayer direct us. Self-justification, on the other hand, prevents us from telling the oftentimes-hard truth about ourselves, leaving us to carry our illusions and half-truths as a heavy burden across our backs. Those words from Abba John very much set the tone for my whole retreat, and I kept coming back to them again and again, checking on my own motivations and truthfulness. An important and lovely gift from an old friend.

When Ben arrived the next morning to review my work, he appeared pleasantly surprised. "This hand is very good, Father, and the proportions of the body are right. But look at the head. The lower half is a bit too narrow, while the top is too big and round." Yes, I did make him look a bit like a Martian, didn't I? "It is a very encouraging start, so now with your second draft you can pay more attention to the head."

As I set to work, I tried in vain to trace the hand Ben had thought was good, but I had neither the light nor the right paper to make that possible. And really, the hand was only moderately good, and so I set out to see if I could do better. Once again it was two and a half hours of work, with my eraser put to prodigious use. Massaging my tired hand, I looked at the finished product with satisfaction. The head was right, the hand at least as good as the first one, and my drawing bore no resemblance to either a snowman or a Martian. I was quite sure Ben would let me move ahead with this one, so I set it aside and went over to the chapel to pick up the little booklet I'd noticed there, on "Preparing for Confession." Father Thorne had arranged to hear my private confession on Sunday morning, just two days away, and I wanted to be sure that I was really ready.

The booklet was produced by the monks of the Hermitage of the Annunciation in New Germany, Nova Scotia, and its full title is *Preparing for Confession: Life in Christ—Healing and Ascetic Therapy*. While the word "therapy" in the title might make one imagine that their approach would reflect a contemporary, humanistic "pastoral care and counseling" perspective, nothing could have been further from the truth.

> Spiritual life is a struggle: it is an invisible warfare against the devil. "We do not struggle against flesh and blood, but against powers, against the rulers of darkness, against spiritual armies of wickedness" (Eph 6.12). Unfortunately, we often understand our sins merely as moral transgressions. In fact, sins are the symptoms of deeper spiritual diseases. These spiritual diseases are called the "passions," which spread like a cancer.[1]

As I sat in the back of the chapel and began to make my way through the booklet, I was aware that I would need to dedicate a good part of the next two days to preparing myself adequately. The introductory material alone ran to seven pages, while the seven-step preparation process provided detailed descriptions of the eight passions, including what were called "symptoms" of each passion or disease of the soul. I saw that this would be slow, careful, and searching work, work I must undertake in light of Abba John's wisdom about the difference between self-criticism and self-justification. I tucked the booklet into my jacket pocket, and wandered out for a good hour-long walk before returning to the chapel for mid-day prayers and the Eucharist.

Here are the Eight Passions, summarized from *Preparing for Confession*:

1. **Gluttony or greed**: Here gluttony includes not only the immoderate desire for food, "but all forms of greed and love for the comforts of life." For me, one unexpected symptom of this passion was said to be "feeling sorry for myself: self-pity."

2. **Avarice and love of power**: While it is seen to have much in common with greed, avarice contains a strong element of the love of control and domination. I was intrigued to see

1. *Preparing for Confession*, p. 4.

one its symptoms identified as the "immoderate attachment to loved ones."

3. **Impurity**: While the Greek word is *porneia*, suggesting that this passion is all about sexual impurity, here it is said to include "all forms of mental dispersion and inattentiveness," with one symptom listed as "letting electronics intrude on your work and relationships."

4. **Anger**: This passion includes both irritability and impatience, and along with such things as outbursts of anger, holding grudges, and bitterness, one of the symptoms of anger is seen to be fear.

5. **Sadness and Jealousy**: Sadness is said to be closely related to jealousy, in that it can spring up when our desires are unmet and we are left envious of those who have what we want. Spiritual sadness, the booklet is careful to note, is not the same thing as clinical depression, for which medical treatment is required.

6. **Despondency**: Also known as *acedia* among the desert fathers and mothers, this passion might best be described as spiritual sloth or *ennui*. While many of the symptoms are what one might expect—weariness, boredom, negligence—interestingly, "undertaking many deeds instead of praying" may also be a symptom of despondency.

7. **Vanity or vainglory**: "people suffering from vanity are the prisoners of the opinion of others about them." This is closely related to pride, and so "seeking honours, power, and praise" is an obvious symptom. So is "refusing to see that I am a sinner."

8. **Pride**: Pride here is related to vanity but is not tied up in desiring the approval of others. In fact, one of the symptoms of pride is said to be "feeling superior and despising others." This suggests that the major difference between vanity and pride is that while the former craves the approval and admiration of others, the latter is concerned only with what one thinks of one's own self.

That afternoon I carefully worked my way through the book-let, taking notes when any of the passions struck me as being present in me, or when the symptoms described sounded familiar. While I could find some echoes of myself in the list of symptoms for each passion, there were a couple of the passions that caught me short. At the end of the afternoon I wrote the following general observation in my journal: "There is no point in asking 'where would I be had this *not* happened,' because it has. And it has wounded me deeply. My wounds are being tended, yet they can also tempt me into salving them with things that aren't marked by grace." What is most instructive in looking back though my journal notes is what I wrote about my reflections on anger: "I am not an angry man, and when I do get angry it tends to be quickly felt and then released." A few days later I would learn different.

Saturday morning found me moving a little more slowly, as the Starbucks didn't open until 7:00 a.m. on weekends. I picked up the local Saturday paper to read while I sipped my coffee, and then made my way back to my cell in anticipation of Ben's arrival. "This draft is much better, Father," he said. "You've got the shape of the head right, and the hand is again really quite good. I think the third one will be the one you'll be able to use." I had of course hoped that Ben would be content with my second draft, so it was with a combination of resignation and determination that I set to work on the third one. That morning I was so fiercely focused on my drawing that time became meaningless: all I recall is finishing up, sitting back with my predictably stiff neck and tired hand, and realizing that I'd hardly been aware of the hours that had passed. And, yes, Ben had been right. A third draft had made all the difference.

I headed out for a long walk, planning to wind my way through downtown Halifax and on down to the waterfront. Before I'd gone too far, I realized that my mind was alive with material that I really needed to get into my journal, and so I found the nearest coffee place and settled in to write. A couple of pages poured out of my pen, most of it having to do with those eight passions I'd been pondering. The wisdom of Abba John was there too, saying, "don't be afraid of self-criticism; fear only self-justification." Almost as a post-script, I added this:

> Here's the thing about all that I just wrote. I spent two and a half hours doing the third draft of my icon, thinking about nothing aside from the lines I was drawing (and re-drawing). Done for the day, I went out for a walk, and everything I just wrote crystallized for me in about ten minutes. The icon, Lord, is doing its work.

Sunday morning as I walked across the quad to the chapel to meet Father Thorne and make my confession, I was deeply aware of my pounding heart and shaky hands. He met me inside the door, led me to the front where I knelt at the altar rail, seated himself on a chair across the rail from me, and placed a Book of Common Prayer in my hands, opened to page 581.

> The Lord be in thy heart and on thy lips, that thou mayest truly confess thy sins to Almighty God.
> I confess to God that I have sinned in thought, word, and deed, by my own fault. And especially . . . I pray to God to forgive me all my sins for the sake of Jesus Christ our Saviour. Amen.

"And especially . . ." That is the place where I needed to speak aloud all the things that I had been pondering and working through over the past two days. Father Thorne wasn't looking for details and long explanations, just that I name the passions that I'd come to realize were troubling my soul and dragging me down. As I named each one, I was aware that my voice was shaking at least as much as my hands. I felt vulnerable, small, broken.

And then after a time of silence, his voice rang with clarity and compassion:

> O most merciful God, who, according to the multitude of thy mercies, dost so put away the sins of those who truly repent, that thou rememberest them no more: Look upon this thy servant, who most earnestly desireth pardon and forgiveness. And forasmuch as he putteth his full trust only in thy mercy, impute not unto him his former sins, but strengthen him with thy blessed Spirit; and whenever

thou art pleased to take him hence, take him into thine everlasting favour; through the merits of thy most dearly beloved Son Jesus Christ our Lord. Amen.

Our Lord Jesus Christ, who hath left power to his Church to absolve all sinners who truly repent and believe in him: Of his great mercy forgive thee thine offences. And by his authority committed to me, I absolve thee from all thy sins, In the Name of the Father, and of the Son, and of the Holy Ghost. Amen.

I realized I'd been holding my breath, but as Father Thorne went on to instruct me to pray and meditate on Psalm 27 throughout the day, I began to draw deep, clean breaths. Taking me by the hands, he lifted me from my knees, looked in to my eyes, and said, "Pray for me, a sinner." My hands felt steadied by his, and as I walked down the aisle to the door, I realized I was at peace. Though it had all taken no more than fifteen or twenty minutes, all the time spent in spiritual and emotional preparation had allowed me simply to name the passions which I recognized were weighing on me—and, in naming them, to strip them of much of their hold.

From there it was on to a very different sort of a day. Church with my sister and her family, an afternoon at their home with my nieces, a good dinner, and then back to my cell by 8:00 p.m. I noted in my journal that, while the day had been really lovely, once the evening came I found myself longing to be back in my cell, back on my own.

Work on the icon progressed. Now that I had a finished draft, the next step was to transfer my sketch onto the wooden board that Ben had prepared for me. The wood surface had been coated with a layer of "gesso," a mixture of chalk, white pigment, and a binder made from rabbit skin. To transfer the image to the gesso, I had to dust the back of my drawing with red tempera powder, fix the drawing paper firmly to the board with the powder against the gesso, and then very carefully retrace the drawing so that the image was imprinted on the board. It worked the same way as carbon paper, with the same challenge of needing to be ever so careful not to smudge the lines. That done, the next step was to etch the image into the gesso, using a fine etching tool. As Ben demonstrated how to do this, his steady hand etched a fine, confident line into the gesso. When I gave it a try, he had me begin with a gently curving line, but I found even a very gradual curve hard to do. It felt like the etching tool had a mind of its own and had decided it liked straight lines a lot more than curved ones. I looked at the tiny curves in my sketch, in the fingernails and around the eyes, and wondered how I'd ever manage to do this. "That's good, Father," said my mentor. "Just go slowly, and don't press too hard. You can go back over a line a few times if need be."

It took me four solid hours that day, and aside from getting up to make a cup of tea I didn't move from my desk. Line by line, curve by curve, I etched the image of Christ into the gesso. My hand ached, and so the tea was as much for the warmth of the mug in my hand as it was for the sake of the drink itself. When I heard the church bell ring for mid-day prayers, I decided to just stay put and pray that brief service on my own. Shortly after 1:00 p.m., I was finished. Aside from a few places where my etching tool had gone astray, I'd managed to etch every line I'd drawn, including those in the eyes and fingers. Now for a walk, to try to shake off the stiffness in my body.

I was no more than five minutes down the road when I became suddenly aware of how angry I was. It was as if my conscious mind had been so utterly focused on etching *this* line and taking care with *that* curve, that my subconscious had grabbed the opportunity to push up an anger I'd not even known was there. It was seething, raw, and poisonous, like nothing I'd ever before experienced, and so I turned right around and went straight back to my cell and to my journal, and began to write. That journal entry begins by sounding measured, reflecting on my emotional exhaustion and the gift of sleep, almost as if the brief walk back had allowed my conscious mind to wrestle down all the anger that my subconscious had pushed up to the surface. But as the five-page entry continues, more of the anger begins to show, and by the final page it is pouring out of me like venom. At the end I wrote simply, "There. That's where the anger is," and put down my pen.

I sat back, feeling drained, with my hands open on my lap. I drew my hands together, and it was as if I could see cupped in them a ball of black poisonous anger. I knew I had a choice. I could either lift that poison to my mouth and swallow it back down where it would surely spread its evil throughout my spirit and destroy me—or I could throw my hands up and let it go. And so I did. I actually raised my hands toward the ceiling, and banished it from me, wordlessly praying as I did. I sat for a few minutes, breathing methodically and deeply, and then rose, put on my jacket, and headed out the door for what was a truly good and long walk.

The Second Week

January 18–24, 2017

The church spends its time trying to change wine into water, because it has not the capacity to believe that Christ turns water into wine.

FROM FATHER GARY THORNE'S SERMON JANUARY 19, 2017

THE ONE LITURGY OFFERED by the King's chaplaincy that follows the contemporary Communion rite of the Canadian Book of Alternative Services is held at 8:00 on Wednesday mornings at the Dalhousie University Multifaith Centre. Called "Wine Before Breakfast," this liturgy gathers a group of a dozen or so students from both King's and Dalhousie for a simple communion service that incorporates a time of conversation in response to the Scripture readings. The liturgy is followed by a shared breakfast at the Centre, and this provided my only regular opportunity to join in conversation with students and begin to attach stories to at least some of the faces that were becoming so familiar to me.

Walking back to my room after breakfast that Wednesday, I began to feel a chill in my body and a lightness in my head that suggested I was probably fighting some sort of a virus. An hour or so later when Ben dropped by to give me my instructions for the day, it was clear that I was fading, and fading fast. Thankfully my icon work for the day was not long—applying gold leaf and then burnishing it with a brush—and, in fact, Ben stayed through to help me with most of it. As soon as he left, I lay down and slept for the hour before midday prayer, and after that it was right back to bed for much of the afternoon. I emerged only at 5:00 for Choral Evensong.

It had been only ten weeks since I'd found myself similarly knocked down by a cold in Collegeville, and again I was reminded to pay attention to what my body was saying. In my journal I wrote, "It feels as if my body is telling me to gear down even more. 'You are emotionally exhausted, Jamie. You've been running on low, low reserves for months, and it is now time to stop.' So it is tea, juice, water, chicken soup, and an even slower pace than last week. Maybe being unable to read much will teach me about just sitting and letting myself begin to get restless? I know my instinct is always to read something, check something, listen to something . . ."

I found reading difficult indeed over those days with my cold, and the book assigned by Father Thorne, *St Silouan the Athonite*, was hardly light reading. The 500-page volume is divided into two parts, the first an account of St. Silouan's life and teaching, the second a collection of the saint's writings compiled by his disciple, Father Sophrony, from the scraps of paper on which he had written. Silouan lived as a monk on Mount Athos in northeastern Greece for forty-five years, dying there in 1938; and canonized in 1987 by the Ecumenical Patriarchate of Constantinople. While I was given much to ponder in the pages of that book, I found that I had no strength to read it during those days I was under the weather.

The next day, my cold was even more set in, and I reflected on that in my journal entry for the morning:

> *Acedia*—"the noonday demon"—When Kathleen Norris begins to unpack this idea in the opening chapter of *Acedia and Me*, she writes of being in a space where time just crawls, and all you can think about is when it will be time to go back to sleep.[1] I've had a few moments like that here, but now that I have this cold, I've been given a real taste of it. The foggy head, the struggle to focus on any reading, and the bone-tired longing to be rested may be temporary, but they are still very real. The chapel

1. Norris, *Acedia & Me*, 1–6.

> liturgies are like glasses of cool, refreshing water punctu-
> ating my long days. Thank you, Lord, for that.

"The chapel liturgies are like glasses of cool, refreshing water," I'd written, and truly they were. On the days when I was trying to pray on my own in my room and couldn't find the right words or was just too restless and unfocussed to sit still, the chapel liturgies did their own work on me. All I needed to do was walk across the quad, settle into a pew in that lovely space, open the Book of Common Prayer, and join my voice with those around me. It might be the eighty or ninety people at Choral Evensong or the University Eucharist, or just the three or four at midday prayer, but it didn't matter because either way the work of prayer was getting done. The prayers of confession, the collects, versicles and responses, would keep returning me to that place of soul-searching humility and truthfulness that Abba John the Little had encouraged. At the same time, I kept hearing an almost stubborn insistence that God was steadfastly at work, often in the most extravagant yet upside-down of ways. I'd hear that every morning in the *Benedictus*—"Blessed be the Lord God of Israel; / for he hath visited, and redeemed his people"—and in the evening in both the *Magnificat*—"He hath showed strength with his arm; / he hath scattered the proud in the imagination of their hearts"—and *Nunc Dimittis*—"To be a light to lighten the Gentiles, / and to be the glory of thy people Israel." And of course there were the Psalms, which spoke sometimes of soul-searching humility and God's steadfastness, yet often, too, of the woundedness of lament and a broken heart. Some days one of those psalms, or even just a verse or phrase of a psalm, would sound in my ear as if it had been written specifically for me.

That first foggy-headed taste of *acedia* fell on Thursday, the day before I was supposed to break the pattern and discipline at King's and head away on an overnight trip to Charlottetown with my sister and her family to watch my niece in her gymnastics competition. By Friday morning I wasn't entirely convinced I should go, so shut down was I by that cold. By lunchtime I'd decided to push through, so I phoned my sister to confirm the time they'd be picking me up—only to hear that my brother-in-law was completely down for the count with a cold even worse than mine, and that my sister was also under the weather. Ah well, off we went anyway, with the two girls in the back seat and my sister and I up front, steadily working our way through a large box of tissues.

I am glad that I chose to push through like that, as it provided a good opportunity for extended conversations with the three of them, and because Molly was particularly delighted that her uncle was there to see her land in first place in the competition. At the same time, it was completely out of sync with the practice I'd been following for the previous ten days. A downtown hotel, dinner out at a very nice restaurant, a king-size bed and a large television mounted on the wall (a television I never even touched), and then in the morning on to the gymnastics meet, where we sat on bleachers, went through cough drops and another box of tissues, and cheered for my niece. Once the awards were handed out, it was back out to the highway for the three-and-a-half-hour drive home. Those two days and all of the driving really laid me low, and I pretty much slept away the next day in my room, having not the energy even to go across to the chapel for the Sunday morning communion service.

I awoke on Monday morning before 6:00 without having even set an alarm, and I felt quite ready to get up and follow my morning walk-and-coffee ritual. I certainly wasn't at full strength, but felt, perhaps, eighty percent. I remember nothing about my ritual that day—whether I read or wrote or emailed, or even how I felt on the walk down to Starbucks—aside from just one thing. As I walked out of Starbucks and looked up the still-dark Coburg Road toward King's, I said aloud, "Well, there goes the best part of my day." What? I really did just say that, didn't I? More than just saying it, I felt it to the very core of my being. It was going to be so long before I could finally go back to bed for the night. This was something quite different from the tiredness born of my cold, for which long naps and cups of hot tea were the proper remedy. This was a real taste of *acedia*, plain and simple.

It turned out to be a very tough day. For one thing, Father Thorne had planned to meet with me that afternoon for our first conversation about how things were going, but he'd sent a message saying our meeting would need to be delayed until later in the week. I found myself almost fixating on resentment about my fractured marriage, which I thought I needed to address in spiritual direction, but now that seemed so far off in the distance. Why is there this resentment, when I had released the anger? I thought it must be more tied up in the passions of sadness and jealousy than in anger, and I so needed to talk it through in spiritual direction.

To further compound my frustration, the next step in my icon writing would be to begin painting, but before I could do that, I was to work on a small practice icon. I had an eight-by-ten-inch painting board with an image of the face of St. Andrew already sketched on it, as well as several other small boards on which to practice blending colors and painting lines. There was Ben's finished version of the St. Andrew icon as well, so that I would have something to try to replicate. Ben showed me how to mix the paints using tempera powder, egg yolk, and water, and he had been careful to explain what sort of texture was needed for the various steps. He had me practice strokes with the various sizes of brushes, attempting to copy his hand in creating fine lines and the washes that would cover much of my icon. "Like this," he'd say as he painted an exquisitely fine black line, beside which my attempt looked more like a sausage. "Good, good. Maybe keep practicing like that before you start on St. Andrew. Good luck, Father."

As I sat at the desk and worked on that practice icon, I felt like I was back again in Grade One. I can see what the teacher wants us to do, and when I look over at the work of the student in the next desk I'm amazed at what she has managed to produce. And then I look at what I've done . . . blah. Try again. Of course that may be a big part of why I was doing this in the first place. It was so outside of my familiar skill set that I couldn't help but be humbled.

Tired and now frustrated, I slept that afternoon, rising for Evening Prayer and a bit of dinner, and then wondering how I would ever make it all the way to Compline at 9:30 that night. The previous week I'd fallen in love with how Compline is done in the King's Chapel, with only taper candles for light and clouds of incense pouring out of Father Thorne's thurible. On Monday evenings a small ensemble of men would lead the music, while on Tuesdays it was a group of women. The chanting was simple and easy to learn yet possessing both beauty and depth. When it came time for the priest to pronounce absolution, I'd been struck by how carefully and intentionally Father Thorne spoke those words:

> May the Almighty and merciful Lord grant unto you pardon and remission of all your sins, [pause] time for amendment of life, [longer pause] and the grace and comfort of the Holy Spirit.

Time for amendment of life was precisely what I was being given there. The previous week Compline had seemed a late-evening balm for my soul, but on this tired and discouraged Monday it felt like a burden, something I had to struggle to attend.

The next morning as I walked out of Starbucks, I had the same feeling again: "There goes the best part of my day." The weather was cold and wet, and so I feared I'd be more or less trapped in my cell for most of the day. The painting of my practice icon went poorly, the end result bearing no resemblance to the one Ben had given me to copy. Well, I thought, it is done, and I've killed off at least a couple of hours. Then I looked at the clock and realized I had been at it less than forty-five minutes, leaving two more hours until midday prayers. I began to think this was all a mistake; not just the icon, but the whole retreat. I wondered whether I should just call it quits, admit defeat, and head home to spend the next three weeks sitting by my woodstove and reading whatever I damn well pleased. This must be the boredom and restlessness of which Father. Thorne had warned me, and I did not like it.

The whole day was like that, with yet another long and agonizing wait until Compline was over so I could just go back to bed for the night. I was tired, disheartened, discouraged, and done.

Interlude

Books, Music, and Two Martinis

TIME FOR A CONFESSION, or at least a measure of full disclosure: the Scriptures, Book of Common Prayer, and Archimandrite Sophrony's *St. Silouan the Athonite* were not the only books I read during my weeks in retreat. Sure, I brought along Elizabeth Zelensky and Lela Gilbert's *Windows to Heaven* and Rowan Williams' *The Dwelling of Light,* both of which would surely count as appropriately "spiritual reading." But on the plane from Winnipeg I'd been reading Bruce Springsteen's 500-page memoir, *Born to Run,* and with several hundred pages still to go I decided to give myself an hour or so every day to continue some more recreational reading. I defined "an hour or so" somewhat generously, particularly over the first ten days when I was struggling to find a space in my solitude—so much so that by the time I was in Charlottetown I found that I really *had* to stop into a used book shop to see what I might find for the next round of my "hour or so" each day. I was drawn to the music section, and settled on *Catch a Wave: The Rise, Fall & Redemption of the Beach Boys' Brian Wilson* by Peter Ames Carlin. Really, Jamie? *That's* what you're going to read in your cell when the deep boredom sets in? Or maybe just when you want to stave off that boredom? So then, perhaps just to assuage a bit of guilt, I grabbed a worn paperback edition of Graham Greene's *The Heart of the Matter,* which at least had the promise of evoking some soul-searching, as Greene's novels almost always do.

Funny thing, though, is that there was actually a good deal of soul-searching in the Springsteen book, and no little room for serious reflection in the story of the troubled life of Brian Wilson. Running in a strange sort of parallel to my own deep work over those hard days, the seemingly unrelated stories of two profoundly gifted musicians spoke to the need we all have for community, self-honesty, mutual support, deep vulnerability and, ultimately, love. Their stories ended up being a good deal more than just distractions or a salve for boredom. To my collection of recreational reading I also added Grevel Lindop's *Charles Williams: The Third Inkling*, a biography of the gifted and controversial novelist, poet, and theologian who, during the years of the Second World War, entered the circle of friends connected to C.S. Lewis and J.R.R. Tolkien in Oxford. I had devoured Williams' novels during my years as an undergraduate and contended with his theological vision during my time in theological college, and so I was interested to dig more deeply into the story of his life. Besides, Williams' theology has had no small influence on Gary Thorne, and was quite explicitly invoked in Gary's pledge included in his first letter to me to "carry some of your burden." For Williams, the bearing of one another's burdens is quite literally possible in that we are created to "co-inhere" one in another, and through what Williams called "substitution" and "exchange" we can—we must—bear one another up.

Lindop's biography of Charles Williams spoke to my need to let myself be cared for, carried, borne up, and loved in all of my wounds, but it also illuminated the complex and even troubling nature of Williams' own broken life. Yet who among us isn't broken? Who among us is in a place to cast the first stone? And why should I be surprised that books of such insight and beauty as Williams' might come from one who bore wounds?

It was the Lindop book that I had with me during my days at the Hermitage of the Annunciation, downloaded to the laptop that

A Kind of Solitude

I *almost* hadn't packed. It was a rare gift that I'd not left it behind in my cell—but more on that a bit further along in my story.

As for music, I had brought along with me to Halifax my aging little iPod, loaded with a small but carefully curated collection of music. There were a few instrumental albums in the mix, among them *Officium*, the lovely and haunting record by the Norwegian jazz saxophonist Jan Garbarek, accompanied by early music vocal group The Hilliard Ensemble. I included two of Bruce Cockburn's albums: *Humans*, which offers some painfully transparent reflections on the dissolution of his own marriage, and *The Charity of Night*, which includes "Pacing the Cage," the song that gave this book its subtitle. Winnipegger John K. Samson also contributed two to my little list; I brought with me his very fine, highly personal, and often melancholy albums *Provincial*, and *Winter Wheat*. *Sanctuary* by Alana Levandoski and psychotherapist James Finley was an important addition to the list, too. A project that for me works more as an audio book with a carefully constructed soundtrack than as a music album, *Sanctuary* traces what its creators call a "healing path" and is informed by the stuff of faith and searching. It was quite perfect for that time and space in my journey.

Music has long served as a soundtrack to my life. I first discovered Top 40 music in the summer of 1971 when my parents replaced an old tube radio at our cottage with a much more current one and allowed me to take the old radio to my room. Record albums soon appeared on my wish lists, and when I was eleven, Neil Young's 1972 album *Harvest* was at the top of my Christmas list. There was something about that creaky voice singing the poignant lyrics of his hit "Old Man" that spoke to my pre-adolescent self, but that song was really just an entry point. Growing up in a safe suburban home I knew nothing of heroin addiction, yet Young's song "The Needle and the Damage Done" spoke volumes to me of what the pain and loneliness of addiction might be. Through my teenage years, into university and right to this day, listening to music provides for me a way to articulate and integrate a full range of emotions, from sorrow and hurt to joy and passion. No wonder, then, that the Psalms, the songs of ancient Israel, have been so important in my spiritual formation. For the most part my iPod just sat quietly on a window ledge in my cell. Most of the time spent writing my icon was in silence, though as I moved more confidently into the use of the paintbrushes I did occasionally put on some music, but always more as a companion to my work than as a background. From time to time in an evening I would put on an album and really listen to it from beginning to end, soaking in the mood and tone and insights offered by the artist.

The album I listened to with the most intention and care was Björk's heart-rending 2015 *Vulnicura*. Written in response to the disintegration of her own marriage, this one reduced me to tears more than just a few times over those weeks. My good friend Steve Bell lent it to me just a week or so before I departed, and while I'd long had an appreciation of Björk's work, I was surprised by how urgently Steve wanted me to take it along on my retreat. Soon enough I would understand. In a review for *The Atlantic*, Spencer Kornhaber writes:

> After a few close listens to *Vulnicura*, it's easy to understand, for once, where the famously inscrutable 49-year-old Icelandic songwriter is coming from. You might even have teared up a few times yourself. There's no mystery to the album, no lyrical code to be cracked, no iPad apps or visual aids or elaborate backstories needed to understand its meaning. *Vulnicura* speaks for itself, and it does so devastatingly.[1]

Devastatingly, as Kornhaber says, but also insightfully, with the chorus of the song "Notget" both piercing my heart and making sense of my pain, helping me to see why walking through five of the most demanding weeks of my life was so necessary. "If I regret us," Björk sings, "I'm denying my soul to grow/ Don't remove my pain/ It is my chance to heal."

And then there were those two martinis. Bless me, Father, for I have sinned. Bless me, Gary, for I never got around to telling you about the martinis. One was on a weekday afternoon, about

1. https://www.theatlantic.com/entertainment/archive/2015/01/bjorks-vulnicura-is-the-definition-of-devastating/384735/ accessed May 17, 2019

two weeks into my time in Halifax, and the other was on the final Saturday before I was to head home. The drink on that Saturday close to the end of my five weeks was planned, an intentional part of my transition toward home. The weekday one, much earlier in my time at King's, was something of an impulse, altogether un-planned and unexpected. I'd headed out after midday prayers on a long walk that would take me to a store close to the harbor that specialized in tartans and other good wool things imported from Scotland and Ireland. I wanted to replace a MacDonald tartan scarf that I'd lost a few years earlier, but when I arrived I discovered that everything in the store was discounted by fifty percent. A clan scarf for me, one as a birthday present for my daughter, and then to top it off, a lovely Irish Aran wool sweater—just the thing to stave off the Halifax damp.

On the way home I noticed a bar that specialized in martinis and thought to myself "why not?"—only to discover it didn't ac-tually open for another couple of hours. Ah, but the place across the street most certainly did. Maybe a little bite to eat there? Something healthy, like a good green salad, with an ice-cold martini on the side. Sure. As I settled in and placed my order, I thought of my grandfather and his daily 5:00 o'clock martini—his gin, mine vodka with an extra olive—and reflected on the degree to which his martini cut against the grain of the church culture in which he spent much of his life. A prominent lay leader in a conservative congregation which would have included many people committed to the temperance movement, enjoying that daily drink just never fussed him, nor did it compromise his solid and serious commitment to faith. I thought, too, of Thomas Mer-ton, who, according to some accounts, was fond of occasionally slipping away from his little hermitage outside of the walls of the Abbey of Gethsemani to head into town for a beer and con-versation at one of the local bars. It felt as if I were in very good company in my infraction of what Father Thorne had established as the working rule for my time of retreat.

Then again, what would he have said had he known? Gary Thorne is both devout and limber, exactly the sort of combination that keeps one from being narrowly "religious." Gary might have scolded me, laughed at me and with me, or just looked silently off into the distance before saying something about how each stumble is little more than an opportunity to turn yet again to God. I don't know. But what I *do* know is that he wouldn't have stopped loving me, respecting me, or praying for me, surreptitious martinis and all.

The Third Week

January 25–31, 2017

ALMIGHTY God, who art afflicted in the afflictions of thy people:
Regard with thy tender compassion those in anxiety and distress; bear
their sorrows and their cares; supply all their manifold needs; and
help both them and us to put our whole trust and confidence in thee;
through Jesus Christ our Lord. Amen.

FROM "GENERAL PRAYERS: FOR THOSE IN ANXIETY,"
BOOK OF COMMON PRAYER, OFFERED AT COMPLINE ON
JANUARY 31, 2017

AT THE END OF Tuesday evening Compline on January 24th,
after my long and discouraging day, Father Thorne stopped me
by the chapel door to see if I might be able to preside at Wine
Before Breakfast the next morning. He was feeling exhausted, he
explained, and would really appreciate a bit of extra time in the
morning. Yes, Gary, of course I can. And I knew I could push
through my own discouragement even if just for an hour or so,
because I knew he must need that extra time if he were asking
me to step in.

As I stepped out of Starbucks the next morning to head toward the Multi-Faith Centre, I looked up at the dawn sky and said
to myself, "This is going to be a good day." What? I just said that,
didn't I? Where is *that* coming from?

It was good to preside at Wine Before Breakfast. The liturgy is not unlike that of my own church community, and as I spoke the familiar words and phrases, I felt myself steady and firm behind the altar, just as I had in my own parish right through those very difficult early weeks. The sharing first of bread and wine and then of breakfast was also good and affirming, my conversations with the students easy and engaging. After breakfast it was back to my room to wait for Ben to come to give me my instructions for the day. I watched his face fall when I showed him my practice icon, but I could hardly fault him for that. I'd not been able to figure out how to shade my paint colors, and my lines were still far too broad. The places at which the very lightest shades were meant to create the effect of light coming from the eyes were badly botched, while what were meant to be fine lines of light paint in the hair looked more like very badly-done highlights. The lovely thing, though, is that at that point we both began to laugh. I admitted that the paint around the eyes resembled sun block, to which Ben replied, "his hair looks makes him look like a sun-bleached California surfer." A holy icon of St. Andrew the surfer dude! My   instructions   for the day involved simply practicing my painting techniques, working to get the lines thinner and develop at least a bit of a knack for shading and blending colors together. I was to do that for an hour at most, and tomorrow Ben said he'd be back with some further practice ideas. I propped St. Andrew the surfer up on the window ledge as a reminder of our laughter.

A friend from Winnipeg was visiting King's for a few days, in part to speak at an event called "Evenspeak"—a lecture series offered on Wednesdays after Choral Evensong—but also to give her teenaged daughter a firsthand look at King's as a possible place to study. With Father Thorne's blessing, the two of us went for a long walk that afternoon, and I found myself telling her that I was beginning to feel lighter than I had in seven months. When I used the word "lighter," it wasn't accidental. That morning after I'd finished my painting practice, I'd gone into the bathroom to clean my brushes in the sink, and when I looked in the mirror it seemed as if there was a real light in my eyes. Oh, I thought, that must just be the sunlight coming in the window playing a trick, so I closed the blind and looked again. Still light. I opened the blind and turned off the bathroom light. There was *still* light. Something was indeed shifting, and so in my journal I expressed both gratitude and my amazement at it all.

> Most people whose marriages come apart don't get to do anything like this. Most people don't have the supports, the church, the friends, the family that I have. I am very fortunate. I am above the surface of the water now, and the lead weights I had tied to my ankles—jealousy, anger, resentment, self-pity, self-loathing—have been turned to balloons. That's grace.

Choral Evensong was lovely, and my friend's Evenspeak lecture on the theme of empathy spoke beautifully and poignantly to what I'd been thinking and praying my way through. I went to bed thankful and content.

I began the next day again feeling really good, greeting the morning skies with the same words as the day before: "This is going to be a good day." My icon work for the morning was to be twofold: first, to take the thinnest brush and outline all of my etched lines of my icon in black; and, second, to practice shading another St. Andrew, this time using colored pencils. The black outlining was for the most part not at all a hard task. At a few points—those eyes and fingers again—I had to be painstakingly careful, but tracing most of the lines was straightforward. Put a little paint on the brush, move it carefully into the etched groove, and let the indented line guide my hand. It was satisfying work, and when it was done I could begin to imagine that I'd actually have a finished icon in a couple of weeks.

When I turned my attention to the colored pencils, however, I was once more right back in grade school. After a few minutes of frustration, I set the task aside and picked up *St. Silouan the Athonite*, but found myself quickly distracted and then just tired. I slept for a while before midday prayers, hoping to return to the feeling of lightness I'd had the day before, yet the afternoon simply felt long and dull. "Right now," I wrote in my journal, "it feels like it will be a long day before I can finally just go to bed."

As it turned out, there were two lovely offerings of grace that day, each of which helped me to break—no, *embrace*—the sense of dullness that was taking hold of me. Father Thorne dropped by my room in midafternoon to confirm the details related to my weekend at the Hermitage of the Annunciation, and I was able to speak with him about my experience of feeling that I was just "pacing the cage." That's a phrase borrowed from the Bruce Cockburn's song that had long spoken to me, but never so much as during these seemingly endless patches of dead time. Father Thorne simply threw his head back and laughed, saying something to the effect of how good it was to be given the time to be that bored. "Roll around on the floor and yell if you need to," he said to me as he pulled on his great beard. "There's no one else living in the building, so no one will notice. If you confront that boredom in the middle of the night, get up and pace the streets. See what the Father might have for you to see." It was for me a funny sort of affirmation, one that said I wasn't simply stalling or grinding slowly off-track, but that I was instead moving in precisely the sort of direction he had envisioned for me. Oh, and his laughter was such a consolation.

That evening my Winnipeg friend Kirsten preached at the University Eucharist, on the healing of a leper and of a centurion's slave (Matthew 8:1–13). In my journal I reflected on her sermon as follows:

> Kirsten dealt with suffering, and talked about how the suffering of the leper allowed him to truly hear—and respond to—what Jesus had said in the Sermon on the Mount. Suffering can allow us to see our need, a need present in all people, but only recognized through experiences of profound vulnerability. To suffer is to be brought into contact with the truth about ourselves. To then be healed is not to forget the wound—not to have it erased as if it were never there—for now one is in a place of knowing *who* to turn to in the face of suffering. Like the centurion, when I see someone in pain, I must go and find Jesus for them.

I then reflected on what that might mean in relation to my experience of the fracturing of my marriage:

> It is wrong to say that God willed the ending of our marriage, and yet God takes it, and turns it into a strange sort of gift for me. The suffering I've felt becomes a point of grace, because I know how deeply I have been hurting. And how many people came to me and saw that? How many saw my pain and ran to find Jesus? So many! I would wish things had not come apart, and I would never wish this experience on anyone. I so wish that life had not derailed in this way. And yet I am alive, and new light is flooding into me. I believe God is making a way for me and in me.

The next day was Friday, the day I was to head to the Hermitage of the Annunciation, and Ben had decided it was time I had a little break from my icon. My attempts at learning to shade and blend colors with pencil crayons had been frustrating and unproductive, and so he said he'd come up with other exercises for me to try on Monday. It was a quiet but satisfying morning, with my usual coffee routine, sung Morning Prayer complete with the Great Litany, and a bit of reading, packing, and walking. Father Thorne picked me up shortly after 11:00, and before we hit the highway for our two-hour drive we stopped at a little fish and seafood place to get some lunch. "I know Fridays are to be fasting days for you, but we'll break with that pattern for this week," he said as we settled into our booth. Ah, fried clam strips, chips, and a salad were a grand way for this prairie boy to be relieved of a fast. Our visit was light and easy, and once we were on the road to the Hermitage we had a mix of Bob Dylan, Leonard Cohen, and Steve Bell as the soundtrack to our conversation about the shape of the Chapel ministry, the changing needs of university students, and the questions Gary had about when it might be time for him to step away from chaplaincy and begin to move toward retirement. It felt as if I were intentionally being given a bit of respite from the soul-searching work I had been doing, and at the same time reminded that I might have some insight to offer regarding the shape of Gary's own ministry and vocation. He didn't come out and say it, but the message was clear: "I value your opinion. You have something real to offer. You are more than your wounds, Jamie."

We arrived at the Hermitage of the Annunciation by midafternoon, and after paying a brief visit to the little chapel—which they called the Temple—I was introduced to the three monks who make their lives there: the Abbot, Father Schema-Igumen Luc, and Fathers Cassian and Nathaniel. Father Luc was extraordinarily gentle and welcoming, and after showing me to my little bedroom he toured me through the rest of the house. In their generously-stocked library Father Luc showed me where books on various topics were shelved: the writings of the church fathers, biblical commentaries, works on the spiritual life from the Eastern tradition. As we came to the last shelf, he said, "And here is the most important book ever written. Do you suppose you know what it might be?" Before I could reply that I assumed it was the Bible, he reached up and pulled down a hardcover edition of *The Little Prince* by Antoine de Saint-Exupéry. Ah, I am going to like this man. Published in 1943, *The Little Prince* was a book Father Luc might have read as a child growing up in France, yet that didn't fully account for his affection for the story. He explained that anytime he came across a copy for sale he would buy it, so that there was always a copy to give to any child who visited the Hermitage. The depth of the story's appeal had somewhat evaded me when I first read it during my undergraduate years, so I vowed to read it again over the weekend.

The Hermitage is located in farm country in rural Nova Scotia and is set on an acreage that includes wooded areas, vegetable gardens, and pasture. A pond is nestled into one section of the woods, beside which a small outbuilding has been constructed for private prayer and retreat. Fathers Luc and Cassian founded their small community in Halifax in 1995, and moved to this rural property in 2003, retrofitting the existing house and barn to better suit their needs and adding the small Temple as the heart of their religious life. The house itself is a fairly large wood frame building of quite recent construction, furnished simply yet comfortably.

With my tour of the house completed, I was left on my own for the few hours before supper. The afternoon was cold but clear and sunny, so I took advantage of that time to walk in the surrounding woods before settling in with *The Little Prince* for a bit before the 5:00 supper. I was summoned to the table, and Father Luc asked if I would enjoy a beer with our meal. Well, if it is on offer, surely that's in keeping with the discipline Father Thorne had set out for me. I agreed that yes, that would be nice, and so Father Nathaniel was dispatched to the basement to fetch three bottles of beer to accompany our meal. Father Cassian was not feeling well that day, so declined the beer and joined us only briefly for the simple but nourishing meal. "Will you help Father Nathaniel with the dishes?" Father Luc asked, though of course it was really less a question and more a cue as to the protocols of the house. Yes, of course—and in short order the two of us were side by side at the counter, chatting easily about his roots in Western Canada and how he'd landed in the Russian Orthodox Church just a few years ago. As we finished, I put on the kettle to make a cup of tea, and as I did I thought I detected a curious look on his face. Father Nathaniel went off toward the library, and a few minutes later as I waited for my tea to steep I heard Father Luc's voice: "Has he gone to his room?" "No, he is making tea." "Oh". Uh-oh.

I hurriedly splashed some milk into my cup, briefly wondering if I might be best just to pour my tea down the drain in case I was breaking a rule regarding some sort of overnight fast. No, I decided, I will just take it to the sitting room by my bedroom and read there for a while. Might as well enjoy this transgression, if in fact it was a transgression. As I flicked off the kitchen light, I realized that, aside from a few nightlights, the house was in total darkness, in spite of it being not quite 6:00 p.m. Okay, then, straight to my little bedroom it is. It was only then that I looked more carefully at the schedule they'd left for me on the bedside table.

> 6:00 p.m.—readings (in cell or scriptorium) & prayer
> 7:30 p.m./8:00 p.m.—beginning of night rest

And why so early? I glanced to the top of the schedule.

3:15 a.m.—end of night rest
4:00 a m.—Jesus Prayer in Temple
5:00 a.m.—Matins in Temple

Needless to say, if your night rest ends at 3:15 in the morning, it makes a good deal of sense to be closing down the house at 6:00 p.m., but it came as rather a surprise to me! Father Luc had mentioned that we would not be praying a full Matins in the morning, but rather would offer a simpler form of prayer in the Temple at 6:00 a.m., preceded by a time of meditation with the Jesus Prayer. I was welcome to join them any time after 5 a.m., he'd explained, so I knew I needed to be in bed quite early. But to my room at 6:00 p.m.? It was going to be a long evening. Thankfully, I not only had *St. Silouan the Athonite* and the borrowed copy of *The Little Prince*, but just that morning had downloaded an electronic copy of Grevel Lindop's biography of Charles Williams to my laptop, and at the last minute had decided to bring it with me. I say thankfully, because there really wasn't a proper light in the bedroom by which to read, so a glowing screen—something I usually don't like for reading—was just the thing.

The morning came early, but it was more than manageable given how early I had been in bed. I was certainly still a little bleary-eyed when I stumbled into the Temple at 5:45 to join Fathers Luc and Nathaniel in meditating on the Jesus Prayer, but with a bit of breakfast and a couple of cups of good, strong coffee, I was soon ready to settle in and do some journaling. As I look back on my entry for that morning, I'm aware of how my longing to be home had begun to shift, from being simply restless to being in a place of preparation for a new beginning. At the core of that longing was a deepening awareness that I would soon need to put the house on the market and find a new place that I could call home.

> January 28—Hermitage of the Annunciation—Saturday morning 7:30. The sun has still not quite emerged, and I've already been to the morning liturgy and had breakfast. The place is comfortable, the setting lovely, the welcome good, but I do feel dislocated. It is a bit of a double-dislocation, really. Not only away from home and

the familiar, but also from the routines and familiarities I've put in place at King's. I'm so aware of my need for touchstones, for a sense of my own space and my own routines. And I don't make such a great houseguest, as I tend to feel I'm in the way or in the wrong place.

It is important to know this about myself, both in general and in anticipation of a move to a new home. The prospect of a move reminds me that I need to honor (ritually?) the significance of leaving our marriage home. Is there a celebration with music, food and drink, and a bonfire out back in early May? Is some sort of prayer ritual incorporated in that? I think the very last thing I need to do after the house is emptied and cleaned is to walk through and bless it with prayer and the sprinkling of water. That's going to be a tearful day.

In terms of my next home, I now know that it needs to somewhere interesting, somewhere I can love and want to be at home in. Not that I should go too far into debt, but I don't want to be so frugal that I land somewhere I'm not happy with. If I am going to be truly "located" there, it will need to be good and right.

It has come to me over these days that I would like to retire from parish ministry in the year I turn sixty. That's only four more years, at which point I will mark thirty-four years of ordained ministry. If I can do that, it would give me more time and space to write, travel, perhaps teach and lecture more, and possibly serve as a mentor and director to younger clergy. I would be able to explore all of these possibilities in a more thoroughgoing way in my sixties, while I still have the energy to do so. Not that I am feeling my age all that much, but I am aware that time is passing and that I cannot delay such dreams endlessly.

Can I make that work, financially? I don't yet know. I don't know what the burden of my mortgage will be. I imagine things might be thin, but my lifestyle can be simple. It is a matter of priorities, which is something I have glimpsed here at the hermitage.

I am ready now—or at least today—to fully forgive in love and then to move on.

> There will be much to do at home to get things ready
> for the sale, including a major cull of my library, finding
> homes for the furniture I will no longer need, the mi-
> nor repairs and touch-ups, and the clearing out of the
> basement. That's the biggest job, what with all that we've
> stored down there over the years. I will begin to take this
> on, step by step, beginning on my first day off once I get
> home. I'll need to contact the realtor about beginning
> the search for my new place, and I will need to make an
> appointment with the bank to arrange financing. Step by
> step, and I will not get overwhelmed because I am ready.

As the day rolled on, I found I was largely left on my own.
In addition to their daily work, study, and prayer, the monks were
busy dealing with a contractor who was there to take measurements
and prepare an estimate for some work to construct a covered link
between the house and the Temple. This was a job required by
the provincial building codes, as the Temple had previously been
registered as a shed, which it most clearly was not. Apparently, a
covered walkway between the two buildings would suffice to have
it deemed a single building. This was a worrying thing both logisti-
cally and financially for the little monastic community.

So it was that I had a quiet morning with another walk in
the woods and plenty of time to read. *St. Silouan the Athonite* was
easier to digest in the daylight, but first I finished off *The Little
Prince*. A confession, Father Luc, and one that I didn't want to pes-
ter you with while you were worrying about the building project: I
really don't understand the appeal of *The Little Prince*. Perhaps I'll
try again in a few years, and maybe someday I'll even have the opportunity to ask someone as wise and gentle as you why so many
people love the story so much. For now it is enough to simply delight in your delight.

Lunch. Rest. Pray. Walk. Read. Vespers. Time for our 5:00
p.m. dinner, again accompanied by a bottle of beer, and marked
by a light and lovely conversation about life in a house without
mirrors. It had been a surprise that morning, to arrive in the bathroom ready to shave and sort myself out, only to realize there was
no mirror. Funny, I'd not really noticed it the night before, but of

course the morning brings the specter of bedhead. But who cares about bedhead when staying with monks who rarely come close to a mirror? "It can be a bit of a shock," Father Cassian remarked with a smile, "to use the washroom at a gas station, and see yourself in a mirror for the first time in months. Where did all the wrinkles and gray come from? And is that peanut butter in my beard?"

I was ready for the evening routine of heading to my room as soon as the dishes were done, forgoing the cup of tea that I longed to make. Back to the Charles Williams biography I went, finding myself pleasantly surprised to discover that by 7:30 I was quite ready to set it down and turn off the light. Morning brought the Divine Liturgy in the Temple, at which we were joined by seven people from the area. At the close of the liturgy we all gathered for coffee and conversation in the house, after which I had time to write in my journal.

> Reflecting on Vespers yesterday and the Divine Liturgy this morning: I felt as if I were visiting a land both beautiful and strange. At some level they have the same liturgical mother tongue as I do, but such a very different dialect, like distant cousins I'd never met and with whom I shared some commonalities, yet there were so many differences. I honor what the monks do here, yet it doesn't draw my heart the way the practice of the Benedictines does. I believe I am unrepentantly a) Anglican; b) reformed *and* catholic; and c) sufficiently indebted to the unconventional evangelical spirit inherited from my great-grandfather S.T. Smith that I always want to seek the *Jesus* way in things. Is the human Jesus visible alongside the exalted Christ?

And then I again wrote of the beginnings of my turn toward home:

> I am ready to go back to my routine in Halifax. Though I am not to "produce" anything, the next two weeks will require a lot of focus on my icon as well as time to write the sermon Gary has asked me to preach on February 9. Next weekend is to be spent at the student retreat, which might be more a burden than a gift. We shall see. Right

now I see these coming two weeks as being a slow transition toward returning home.

Indeed, those weeks were that slow transition. Bit by bit Father Thorne was having me engage more with the students, suggesting I accept a dinner invitation to one of their homes and encouraging me to prepare to be fully engaged with all of the students who would attend the retreat. Even his invitation to preach at the University Eucharist during my final few days there felt like an invitation to resurface from the kind of solitude I'd been engaging in, and to fully take hold of my priestly calling. Meanwhile my icon still needed a good deal of work, and Ben seemed confident he could help this neophyte learn to shade and blend colors. A tireless coach is that Ben.

The Fourth Week

February 1–7, 2017

MAY the Almighty and merciful Lord grant unto you pardon and remission of all your sins, time for amendment of life, and the grace and comfort of the Holy Spirit. Amen.

FROM AN ORDER FOR COMPLINE, *THE BOOK OF COMMON PRAYER*

The sung Compline liturgies held on Monday and Tuesday evenings at 9:30 were among the most treasured of all of the Chapel services I attended over those weeks. Even on the days that I could hardly find the courage to stay awake for the long stretch of time between the end of Evening Prayer and the beginning of Compline, once I walked through the doors of the chapel I was at peace. But for the small beeswax tapers each of us held, we were in darkness, and the warm glow of the flames in the midst of the darkened chapel spoke volumes to my soul. The chanting was lovely, the smell of the incense deeply grounding, the words of the liturgy at once familiar and new. I particularly loved the way Father Thorne always spoke the absolution, placing special emphasis on that phrase I most needed to hear: "time [pause] for amendment of life."

Time: the way his voice punctuated that one word spoke to a space of deep longing within me. I had read, prayed, and heard that absolution many, many times, but had not before noticed the weight of that one phrase. As I'd realized early on in my retreat, time for amendment of life was precisely what I'd been given here, amendment in the sense not only of learning to speak in confession the truth of my sin and failing, but also of having my soul restored and beginning to learn tend my own wounds. Those things, surely, are signs of an amended life. Or better, of an *amending* life, for who of us is ever done with that work?

During these days *St. Silouan the Athonite* sat largely untouched on the edge of my desk, its 500 pages weighing heavily on me. I'd had little trouble reading Part I of the book, in which Archimandrite Sophrony offers an extended account of his mentor's life and teaching, but the pages and pages of St. Silouan's own writings collected from scraps of paper were considerably more challenging. Again and again, St. Silouan returns to a small handful of themes, largely drawn from an asceticism so rigorous as to be all but unimaginable. By his own account, St. Silouan wept almost ceaselessly for the sins of the world, and battled with demons in a way deeply reminiscent of the accounts of the Desert Fathers and Mothers of the fourth and fifth centuries. St. Silouan's writings, though, struck me as lacking the warmth and humor that characterize many of the stories and sayings of the ancient Desert Fathers, and many times I really had to struggle to make sense of his teaching. Some fifteen years into his time as a monk of Mount Athos, Siloaun found himself dispirited and exhausted. Trying to kneel before an icon of Christ, he felt himself confronted by a demon. Crying out in prayer, he recounted hearing in his heart the message, "The proud always suffer from demons." It was when he asked God how he could overcome that pride that heard the words that he believed he received directly from God: "Keep thy mind in Hell and despair not."

As I tried to contend with the meaning of such a startling message, I came to see it as a considerably more severe version of the teaching of Abba John, in that to "keep one's mind in Hell" is about embracing the deepest humility through an extreme form of self-criticism. This is then held in a kind of tension with the instruction to "despair not" because God is good and can be trusted with the salvation of the world. But the intensity of St. Silouan's language and austerity remained quite foreign to me.

During the first few weeks of my retreat I had wondered why Father Thorne was so determined that I should read this book. On that first day, when he handed me his battered copy, he muttered something about how we would discuss it as the weeks went by, and so I made very careful notes in the back pages of my journal in preparation for those conversations. Aside from the occasional query from Father Thorne as to how my reading was going, however, we didn't really engage in any discussion of the book. Over those weeks, I had been anchored in the familiar language of the Book of Common Prayer, the ceremonial of the liturgy, the chapel hymnody, and the plainsong psalm chants, all of which spoke to my home in the English church tradition. To this Father Thorne had added the reading from St. Silouan, a Russian Orthodox monk and mystic, as well as the writing of an icon, and my visit to the Hermitage of the Annunciation—all of which drew me out of my familiar Western Christian formation and into the theology, spirituality, and worldview of the Eastern Church. It was as if I'd been handed a different set of lenses through which to look, lenses which tilted things at an unusual angle and challenged me to patiently let my eyes learn slowly to adjust to this strange and ancient horizon. Not, mind you, for the sake of abandoning the tradition in which I was at home, but rather to learn to see and appreciate it anew. Perhaps this was Father Thorne's intention in having me read St Silouan—and what a lovely bit of providence it was that Father Ingalls had chosen to cite Abba John the Little in that sermon so early in my time at King's, offering me yet another Eastern voice that I could hear with such clarity and conviction.

I must also say the manner in which St. Silouan steadily emphasized the love of the enemy as being the thing most needful in the life of prayer transcended the differences between the Eastern and Western traditions. I did have to wonder just who it was that this Athonite monk might have considered a true enemy, living as he did in his Russian Orthodox monastery in the spiritual center of Orthodox Christianity. Did St. Silouan mean those monks who irritated him (as happens in any community of human beings), or maybe those with whom he experienced significant theological differences? Perhaps he was thinking of those who didn't live up to the same high standard of asceticism by which he lived his life of devotion? It is impossible to know, of course, yet his insistence upon loving the enemy spoke to me in a powerful way. Enemy is a strong word, and one that I'm not naturally inclined to use for anyone in my world, but I can think in terms of those with whom I have significant differences or misunderstandings and those who have caused me hurt. And I had been hurt. In my first week of this retreat I had been confronted with my need to let go of the poisonous anger I'd not known was buried so deep within. Now this Russian saint was insisting that I must not only release my anger but also make the choice to hold love for the person who had caused this hurt, and do that knowing that I too have been guilty of causing hurt. That realization helped to make real sense of what St. Silouan meant by an "enemy," and what such a love actually requires of me.

Thanks to Ben's patience and coaching, I did manage, more or less, to get a feel for the challenge of working with shading paint colors, and slowly but surely the work on my icon progressed. On the Friday morning before we set out for the student retreat, Ben dropped by my cell accompanied by a graduate student who was also learning to write icons as a spiritual practice, and I found I was actually quite pleased to show my progress to both of them. "Well, Father," Ben said, "That's really very good"—to which I said something about not being entirely pleased with some of the shading I'd done, and how intimidated I was to set about the work on the eyes. Turning to Ben's companion, I remarked on how many, many hours it had taken me to get to this point—to which he replied, "But how wonderful to sit for all those hours in the presence of the face of Christ!" True enough; St. Andrew the surfer dude notwithstanding, I estimate that between the draft drawings, practice icons, painting exercises, and the icon itself, by that point I'd spent some thirty-five hours at that desk, with another six or eight to go. While I had prayed over my work every day, I smiled now at this new insight about it all having been done in the presence of Jesus' gaze. Lovely.

Attending the student retreat moved me even more fully toward thinking about making a transition to home, as I was now quite clearly expected to fully engage the students and participate in all the weekend had to offer. While Father Thorne had originally described it as "an intense weekend with forty students or so" it turned out to be more like a hundred students, plus another fifteen leaders, facilitators, and friends. A good percentage of the students weren't part of the regular Chapel community, yet the reputation of these retreats—held once in the fall and then again in the winter—was such that even students of no religious faith found them attractive. Held at a comfortable camp facility a couple of hours from Halifax, the winter retreat offered an opportunity to get away from the damp and often gray city to spend a couple of days with good friends in clean, white snow under very clear blue skies. There were scheduled sessions with a guest speaker, Dr. Roberta Barker, who gave a series of four lectures, entitled "The Old Flame: Virgil, Beatrice, and Love," which was highly engaging and challenging. There was also shared Morning and Evening Prayer, scheduled to coincide with lectures or meals, and lots of time to walk, take part in outdoor activities, visit, read, or just nap by the fire. Last thing at night before the lights went out in the main lodge, we were invited to walk to a little inlet on the lake, congregating, some on one side and some on the other, to chant Compline antiphonally by candlelight across the ice. In addition, at 6:30 on each of the mornings there was a sung celebration of the Prayer Book Eucharist out on the frozen lake, complete with full vestments, incense, a sermon, and a good deal of time spent on our knees in the snow. Though not exclusive, this liturgy turned out to "belong" largely to the active Chapel community, and so was attended by about thirty of us. To find myself part of a group of thirty people willing—no, *happy*—to gather on the ice to celebrate the Eucharist before the sun had even risen was a remarkable experience.

The Fourth Week

A few days prior to the retreat, I had begun to read *The Heart of the Matter*, the novel I'd purchased in Charlottetown, and was glad to have a nice long stretch of reading time at the retreat. Sitting in the lodge close to the fire, I was surrounded by a handful of students similarly immersed in their books, interrupted only occasionally by someone curious to see what I was reading.

The Heart of the Matter is one of what critics identify as Graham Greene's "Catholic novels," in which Catholicism figures almost as a character in itself. Like the whisky priest in *The Power and the Glory*, or the architect Querry in *A Burnt-Out Case*, Major Scobie (the protagonist of *The Heart of the Matter*) struggles to make sense of his Catholic faith in the context of the sin and struggles of his life. As a reader of these novels, I always find myself identifying with these characters and holding out hope for some sort of grace and redemption, even as their lives fray and their decisions betray the profoundly self-justifying burden they are choosing to bear. There is a key scene in *The Heart of the Matter* in which Scobie confronts within himself what he calls "the ruthless dictator" that lies within his heart, the self which had led him to wish that the passenger ship on which his wife was sailing would be sunk at sea so that his own affair with his new lover would not be interrupted, his temporary happiness not be lost.[1] Greene's artistry draws the reader in so deeply that, as Scobie briefly entertains that wish, it struck me as entirely reasonable, even desirable that this should happen—and then, when Scobie quickly turns in horror to confront what is lying in his heart, it pulled me up short. What "ruthless dictator" might yet be working in my own heart? How could I so easily be drawn to identify with Scobie's wish that his wife would die at sea, a thousand other passengers going down with her? I lifted my eyes to stare out the window of the lodge, asking myself whether I had yet taken to heart the fullness of my need to let go of all self-justifying ways of thinking, and to honestly confront the spaces within me that needed healing and restoration. In her book, *Traveling Mercies*, Anne Lamott explores the idea, "that forgiveness is giving up all hope of having had a

1. Greene, *The Heart of the Matter*, 190–92.

different past,"[2] and it strikes me that framing forgiveness in this way involves moving beyond the regrets and resentments that give the heart's ruthless dictator room to maneuver. This is where I am, this is what has happened, and nothing can create a different past. It is time to let go.

As the retreat drew to a close, I began thinking that if I were to finish my icon in time to take it home, it would require some serious attention. Once settled back in my cell in Halifax, I set to the task of shading in and around the eyes, adding the thinnest of lines of white to the hair, aware when I was finished that I'd come a long way since my disaster with poor St. Andrew. I wasn't sure I'd been entirely successful with my shading, but Ben was endlessly encouraging, and even assured me that he'd lend a hand with the eyes if I really needed help. I was getting ever so close to finishing, and the icon was looking better than I'd imagined it ever could.

On one of those afternoons I discovered that I was out of energy for reading, much less for journaling or even thinking, so I determined it was a good time for a solid nap. I decided to switch on the radio on my little iPod to see whether there was something on CBC to lull me to sleep—only to discover that the program being aired was about to bring me yet another layer of insight. It was a discussion of the work of the noted anthropologist Margaret Mead, who apparently had once commented that people often have three marriages over the course of their lives, very often with the same person. The first marriage is about passion and romance, the second is for the provision of the security and stability needed for raising a family, and the third is for companionship. Oh, I suddenly realized; it is this prospect of a long companionship that I feel I've lost. All of the shared work on our house and yard, all the meals we had prepared for one another, the shared values around what mattered and what didn't: those things were all evidence of a companionship I had assumed would only deepen over the years. As I digested Mead's observation, I realized that I didn't feel so much angry or resentful, but instead sorrowful over losing what might have been. In the past several years it had seemed to me

2. Lamott, *Traveling Mercies*, 213.

there had been such promise for the next chapter—for the third marriage, so to speak—and I needed now to learn to truly grieve the loss of that promise.

Interlude

Communion and the Book of Common Prayer

Immersed so deeply in the liturgies of the Book of Common Prayer for all those weeks, I found I had to remind myself that many people experience this book as overly penitential, stern, and even condemning. Why, they wonder, is the language of the confession in the service of Holy Communion so blunt about our "manifold sins and wickedness"? Why, in the prayer that immediately follows communion, do we still need to hear of our need to have our offenses pardoned? More vivid still is the prayer known as the "Prayer of Humble Access", that immediately precedes the sharing of communion:

> WE do not presume to come to this thy Table, O merciful Lord, Trusting in our own righteousness, But in thy manifold and great mercies. We are not worthy So much as to gather up the crumbs under thy Table. But thou art the same Lord, Whose property is always to have mercy: Grant us therefore, gracious Lord, So to eat the Flesh of thy dear Son Jesus Christ, And to drink his Blood, That our sinful bodies may be made clean by his Body, And our souls washed through his most precious Blood, And that we may evermore dwell in him, And he in us. Amen.

Even in the Eucharistic prayer itself we hear the priest pray for God "mercifully to accept this our sacrifice of praise and thanksgiving, most humbly beseeching thee to grant, that by the merits and death of thy Son Jesus Christ, and through faith in his blood, we and all thy whole Church may obtain remission of our sins, and all other benefits of his passion." *Humbly* beseeching, still praying for remission of our sins—in the middle of the prayer in which we are giving thanks and blessing the bread and wine for communion?

All this talk of unworthiness and sin will lead many to protest: aren't we created in the image of God, and in Christ claimed as the beloved children of God? And, if that is true, then why are we being made to dwell repeatedly upon our lack of worth? Assuming that the penitential language of the BCP is mired in some imagined and relentless sixteenth-century guilt, many Canadian Anglicans have happily set the old prayer book aside in favor of the 1985 Book of Alternative Services. But I suggest that such an either/or stance entirely misses the spirit of the Prayer Book's Communion liturgy.

When I first entered the Anglican Church as a university student, it was in the context of a parish church that used exclusively the Book of Common Prayer, and it was there that I first came to appreciate both the beauty of its language and the power of its proclamation of the assurance of grace. To be sure, my three decades of ordained ministry have been spent in parishes that, for the most part, have not used the Book of Common Prayer, but it remains my Anglican mother tongue, and one which I spoke fluently during those five weeks with the King's College Chapel community. Far from feeling pushed to my knees and battered with crippling shame and guilt, I experienced those liturgies as providing the space I needed to confront my failings, sin, and shame in a manner very much in the spirit of Abba John's call to take on the light burden of honest self-criticism. Day after day I would walk through the doors of that chapel, tell the truth of my own brokenness and fears, breathe deeply the air of forgiveness, and come to the table ready to "feed on him in thy heart by faith with thanksgiving."[1] Day after day I would walk out through those

1. From the words for administering the bread from the Book of Common Prayer, the full text of which is: "The Body of our Lord Jesus Christ, which was given for thee, preserve thy body and soul unto everlasting life: Take and eat this in remembrance that Christ died for thee, and feed on him in thy heart by faith with thanksgiving." (BCP p. 84)

chapel doors knowing that I had again been taken by the hands and raised from my knees reconciled, ready to do a little more work on my icon, try yet again to make sense of *St. Silouan the Athonite*, write in my journal, or maybe simply face the boredom of my cell. It was all part of the light burden I was learning that I needed to carry.

The King's College Chapel community knows something about all of this. They know a thing or two about what it means to sink to your knees and to embrace the robustly penitential soul-searching texts of the liturgy, both spoken and sung, and they don't shy away from that. They have come to learn that for every penitential note that is sounded in that liturgy, there is a corresponding note of grace, pardon, and promise. In the "Prayer of Humble Access", for instance, our admission of being unworthy is immediately followed by the phrase, "But thou art the same Lord, Whose property is always to have mercy," while the first words the congregation hears after the confession and absolution are what are known as "the comfortable words," beginning with "Come unto me all that labour and are heavy laden, and I will refresh you." So no, that Chapel community doesn't shy away from the language of penitence, because they also know that the journey of the soul held in that communion liturgy will just as surely raise them again to their feet to sing a closing hymn with heads raised and eyes alight.

In their company I did that day after day after day. And it was good.

The Fifth Week

February 8–14, 2017

Neither was it mine adversary, that did magnify himself against me;
for then I would have hid myself from him.
But it was even thou, my companion,
my guide, and mine own familiar friend.
We took sweet counsel together,
and walked in the house of God as friends.

PSALM 55:13–15, PRAYED AT EVENSONG,
FEBRUARY 10, 2017

ENTERING MY FIFTH AND final week, the transition from my time of retreat was fully underway. The depth of my solitude had been brought to a close through my participation in the student retreat, and while I was still spending most of my time alone, my level of engagement with the Chapel community was increasing. Contrary to what he had originally set out for me, Father Thorne had asked me to preach at the University Eucharist on February 9, and this indicated to me that he thought it time that I begin to really take hold of my priestly ministry.

The Gospel text for the service was Matthew 13:24–30, the parable known as "the wheat and the tares." I began my sermon by recounting an incident from some thirty years earlier when I was a theological student in Toronto, and was living in an apartment on the second floor of one of those typical Toronto brick houses along Danforth Avenue. My landlord lived on the main floor, and he used the back door and back yard, while we were to use the front door and care for the front yard. When spring arrived, I went to work on the yard, tearing up what to my eye looked like the brittle, thorny, stick-like branches of some sort of dead shrub. Later that day I discovered I'd torn out raspberry canes, much to my landlord's dismay. It was a good jumping off point for the parable, and as I brought my sermon to its eventual close, I offered the following:

> Back for a minute to my experience with the raspberry canes. As I worked at this sermon, it occurred to me that I'd actually lived out a kind of parable there in my little yard in Toronto. I'd seen only a tangle of dry, thorny sticks, which I took to be dead, and so tore them up with all of the zeal of an inexperienced gardener. A seasoned gardener would have recognized what they were, and known what to cut down, how to work the soil, what fertilizer to dig in, and when the new growth began to break through the earth a seasoned gardener would have known what to prune back and what to let grow. It was all too easy for me in my unseasoned zeal to see only dryness, thorniness, and deadness, and quite frankly it remains all too easy to see dryness, thorniness, and deadness in the things and the people all around me, and sometimes in my own self, too. But as I pick up the spade and turn go to work, if I'm attentive I will hear the voice of the Master Gardener, telling me to back away; to let him lead me in doing a different kind of work, so that new shoots might spring forth from what seems dead. Watch, this Gardener says to me. I did it definitively with the broken stump of the tree of Jesse, and I can and will do it again and again and again. You see only death and dead ends, but I have dwelt amongst you for the sake of the salvation of the last and the least and lost and the little; even for the raising of the dead. Put down that spade, Jamie. And watch.

In retrospect I realized I was largely preaching to myself, about the way that the Gardener had been carefully pulling the thorns and weeds—the anger, the resentment, the shame and self-doubt—that had grown within me. Pulling them at just the right time, mind you, and tossing them into the burning pile, all the while telling me to leave them there and accept the grace of a new beginning. Under the influence and tutelage of the theologian Robert Farrar Capon, I'd been preaching this for years, but there in that chapel it rang with such freshness and insistence.

Over those closing days it had become quite clear that my icon would indeed be completed in time to take home with me. With a little bit of help from Ben on the very finest lines in the eyes, the work was done just in time for the light spray varnish to dry before I was to take it across to the chapel for a blessing at Evensong on February 10. That was very moving, to have Father Thorne pray strong words of blessing over the icon and then to have the students come forward to reverence the face of the Christ over which I'd labored, prayed, struggled, and even laughed so much over those weeks. My icon was then left on the altar for the four days until I departed, right alongside the one that Ben had been writing in parallel with mine. I learned that it is the tradition to leave a newly-written icon on the altar for fully forty days, and while that wasn't going to be possible for mine, it was consoling to know that I was at least partially participating in that tradition. It was also lovely to be able to slip into the chapel over those days, just to see it there in a space long committed to prayer and the sharing of communion.

Yet even during that Evensong marking the end of my icon-writing, I was again made aware of my need to continue the work of grieving and inner restoration. Of the four psalms we prayed that evening, the verses of one of them leapt off the page, catching in my throat and making my heart skip a beat.

> Neither was it mine adversary,
> that did magnify himself against me;
> for then I would have hid myself from him.
> But it was even thou, my companion,

my guide, and mine own familiar friend.
We took sweet counsel together,
and walked in the house of God as friends.

(Psalm 55:13–15, *The Book of Common Prayer*)

The next morning I wrote the following note in my journal: "All I can say is yes. That's that hardest thing, alright." Thankfully, this translation of Psalm 55 very quickly turns to the response I most needed to ponder, as the next verse had us pray,

As for me, I will call upon God,
and the LORD shall save me.
In the evening, and morning,
and at noon-day will I pray, and that instantly;
and he shall hear my voice. (Psalm 55:16–17)

As it turns out, there is actually a verse missing, one omitted by the editors of the 1962 Canadian edition of the Book of Common Prayer, which was part of their editorial practice at the time.[1] This is not something about which I'm typically very happy, as I'm inclined to believe that part of the gift of the psalms comes in their oftentimes-blunt rawness. This time, though, that editorial practice provided me with a little gift, turning me toward God—morning, noon, and night—as the one source of the deep restoration I so needed in the depths of my heart and soul. Had that questionable editorial practice not informed the editors of the 1962 book, the next verse to be prayed would have been:

Let death come hastily upon them,
and let them go down quick into hell:
for wickedness is in their dwellings, and among them.

I don't want or need to pray death and hell on anyone, and particularly not on this person with whom for years I took "sweet

1. The Psalter of the 1962 Canadian *Book of Common Prayer* actually omits Psalm 58 entirely, and in other psalms removes verses that the editorial committee apparently considered problematic for public worship, daily prayer, or both. Psalm 137, for instance, is shorn of its closing three verses (7–9), which effectively shifts it from being an imprecatory psalm to a straight up lament.

counsel," quite literally walking "in the house of God as friends," and without whom the seeds for what was to eventually become saint benedict's table would never have been planted. No, I needed the acknowledgment of my grief's source offered in verses 13 to 15, and then that reminder to simply "call upon God." It was enough.

While Father Thorne's original plan called for me to spend Sundays with my sister and her family, the weekend at the Hermitage and the student retreat meant that I'd not really seen them since our whirlwind trip to Prince Edward Island during my second weekend. This final weekend, then, was an important one in terms of family. My nieces were keen on seeing the movie *La La Land*, so after attending church together that morning we grabbed a quick lunch and headed into the theater for an experience about as different from my weeks of solitude as can be imagined. And then it was back to their home for a nice dinner accompanied by a good bottle of wine, after which I borrowed their car to go and do some grocery shopping for an event happening the next evening.

Monday February 13 was to be my last night in Halifax, and the previous week Father Thorne had come up with a way for me both to say my farewells and to offer a gesture of thanks to the Chapel community. I was to prepare a dinner for thirty-five or forty people, and he would take care of making a salad and providing some wine. I worked out a plan for a Moroccan-inspired stew, and I would provide both a vegetarian version and one with chicken. My shopping list: chicken thighs, onions, garlic, ginger, peppers, dates, sweet potatoes, chickpeas, stewed tomatoes, Kalamata olives, lemons, organic chicken and vegetable stocks, thick yogurt (for topping), and lots of flat bread. Father Thorne would bring the spices from home in the morning—cumin, coriander, cinnamon, cayenne, and paprika—along with two large stew pots. Somehow I managed to get everything that needed to be chilled into the little bar fridge in my room, and with my plan firmly in view I headed to bed.

I was up shortly after 5:45 to get ready for my morning walk and coffee. Looking out the window I realized there was more than a little snow blowing around, though it was still dark and difficult to see how much had actually fallen. A fair bit, it turned out, making my walk more challenging than usual. By the time I arrived at my destination it was really blowing, and so I was glad to see that the lights were on at Starbucks. As I came through the door and began to shake the damp snow off my backpack, the young woman at the counter said, "I can't believe we're even open. I just heard the buses are canceled and all of the government offices are closed for the day." But you're open long enough for me to have my coffee? "We're open until my manager phones and tells me to close," she replied, already handing me my large cup. Thank goodness.

The trek back from coffee an hour later was even tougher, and when I went across the quad to the chapel for Morning Prayer no one was there and the doorway was blocked by a couple of feet of drifted snow. Back to my cell, then, where I caught the 8:00 news and weather on the radio. Everything was closed down for the day, in what was predicted to be one of the worst blizzards of the year, if not the decade. So much for my dinner, I thought. Well, someone will be able to put all these groceries to good use.

An hour or so later I heard something thump against my window. The blowing snow was so wet it had stuck on the windowpanes, making it impossible to see into the quad, so I wasn't at all sure what might have caused the thump. Then there was a second thump, and this time I could see that it was a snowball hitting the window. It seemed someone was at the locked outside door, trying to get my attention—and, sure enough, when I opened the door into the quad there stood Father Thorne, bundled in winter hiking gear and holding out a big stew pot in each hand. "The spices are in this one," he shouted into the howling wind. "Do you need anything else?" "A good, big, sharp knife?" I ventured, not quite believing he was standing there. "I'll be right back," he said, and then turned to tramp back along the path he'd cut through the drifting snow.

He's kidding, right? Who am I cooking this meal for, when the whole city is closing down? When he arrived back with the knife, I basically said as much. "No, no, they'll be here. Plan for thirty." And then back into the blizzard he trudged.

A good part of my afternoon was spent in the student kitchen, peeling and chopping, and then browning and simmering the ingredients in two batches, all the while aware that I was commandeering the stove designated for use by resident students. Whenever someone arrived in the kitchen, I'd get a puzzled look. "Sorry I'm kind of taking over here, but Father Thorne is having me prepare a meal for the Chapel community," I'd say. "Oh, Father Thorne . . . of course," was the typical reply, leaving no question that they knew to expect the unexpected from their campus chaplain. The Eucharist was set to begin at 5:00, but at 4:30 there was still no sign of the blizzard abating. I slogged across the quad to the common room where we were to have the meal, and discovered Father Thorne madly chopping tomatoes, onions, and cucumbers for his salad. "Grab a knife," he said, and then asked, "Have you seen anyone around?"

No, no, I haven't. And there's a huge snowdrift blocking the chapel entrance. Those words were hardly out of my mouth when a student walked in to see if he could help with anything.

"Get a shovel and clear a path to the chapel," Father Thorne instructed, and out the door the student gamely walked.

Gary, do you think anyone is actually going to be there?

"Oh, they'll be there," he replied. "Get chopping!"

He sent me over to the chapel just a few minutes before 5:00, as I was to preside at the Eucharist and needed to get myself vested. As I pushed the door open, I was stunned to see about twenty-five people awaiting my arrival, and by the time the liturgy began we were up to thirty. I actually have no memory of the liturgy or of sermon, just a strong impression of the presence of those folks who'd managed to hike their way in through the snow. To be sure, some actually lived in residence at King's, but most were from off campus, and one person had even snowshoed the three kilometers from her apartment.

When the Eucharist ended, we moved to the common room, and together feasted against the cold and dark of that storm. At the end of the meal Father Thorne asked me to speak to the community about my experience at King's, and as I began I realized I needed to say something about what had brought me there in the first place; all the students knew was that I was a priest from Winnipeg who had come to spend five weeks on a contemplative retreat. I didn't go into much detail, but I did say that I was coming out of a very tough year, marked by deep sorrow, loss, and grief, and that at the very lowest point in the year Father Thorne had reached out to me in friendship. Six months after he first reached out, that friendship had landed me in their midst, in a posture of openness to God's grace and mercy. I then spoke about the hospitality I'd received in the chapel—this stranger who kept coming to liturgy after liturgy, day after day, week after week. It didn't matter if it were a small gathering at noon or the larger crowd who attended the weekly Choral Evensong or University Eucharist, there was always a space for me in the pews—always a greeting, a smile, perhaps a word of encouragement. That's what I'd experienced, and I'd watched as other strangers had been offered the same gentle welcome.

When I finished speaking, Father Thorne stood up and said, "Jamie, you came to us with a broken heart. This is a community that always has room for the broken-hearted, because every year in Holy Week we walk with the broken-hearted Jesus. And we know his mother's broken heart as well—'a sword shall pierce your own soul also.'" Heads nodded around the room, in acknowledgement of that truth. Always room for the broken-hearted.

By the time our community dinner and all the conversations were finished, the blizzard had largely died down. It was soon going to be time to sing Compline together, so after dropping a few things off in my cell, I made my way back across the quad toward the chapel. The wind was still blowing, and the snow was deep and wet, but the worst of the storm was over. A student came up to walk beside me, his parka hood pulled tight around his face. "Well, Jamie, it looks like we're going to sing Compline outside under the tree." "Will," I said to him, "maybe *you're* going to sing Compline under the tree, but I'm going to sing it inside with the rest of the community." Then I opened the chapel door, only to see Father Thorne bundled up with his jacket under his cassock. "We're praying outside tonight, my brother," he said, and soon about twenty of us were processing out the door with candles in our hands, candles that stayed lit in the wind for all of three seconds. As we processed into the quad, we bumped into the President of the University, who was finally able to take his dog out for a bit of a walk after the long stormy day. "You have to be kidding me," he said, looking both a little shocked and completely intrigued. A minute later he was back in the quad, having put his dog safely back in his lodgings. "I just couldn't pass this up," he said, still shaking his head in wonder.

We divided into two sides so we could chant the liturgy back and forth to each other, and the whole time I'm just thinking, "Oh Gary, you're just having us do this because you can. You're creating a memory here." I shivered, wishing I'd put on my new wool sweater, because even though it was only four or five degrees below freezing, there was a chill, Maritime damp in the air.

Two thirds of the way through the liturgy, we came to the prayers and confession. The young woman leading us intoned, "Let us pray," and we all dropped to our knees in the snow; wet snow that immediately soaked our knees with icy cold. We began to chant:

> Lord, have mercy upon us.
> Christ, have mercy upon us.
> Lord, have mercy upon us.

Still kneeling, we chanted the Lord's Prayer, and then the set of responses. We spoke the confession—"time for amendment of life"—and received absolution, followed by the second set of responses. Still kneeling.

Then the young woman who was leading the intercessions called us into prayer. "This night we pray especially for those in our city who have no shelter, no place to call home. Those sleeping in bus shelters and doorways, and under bridges." And it came to me: *that's* why we're doing this. There's a prayer sometimes said before meals that says, "make us ever mindful of the needs of others." On our knees in the cold, wet snow, we were indeed mindful of the needs of people who that night would be sleeping rough. *That's* why we needed to sing that liturgy out in the cold darkness—so that we'd not forget, not take our own warm spaces for granted, not fail to walk with a deep awareness that the homeless and the broken are also our brothers and sisters.

Compline in the snow was truly a memorable way to cap off what had been a most memorable Eucharist and community meal, which was itself capping off a most extraordinary five weeks. I'd paced the cage of my solitude, learning how deeply I needed to accept—really and truly accept—God's deep forgiveness for all the failings that had brought me there in the first place. Having come to accept that forgiveness, I realized that I needed to keep pacing and pacing and pacing, toward the next step: the step of acceptance, acceptance at a depth where my burden truly could be released. There had been—would still be—a lot of darkness in my pacing, because acceptance like that is hard. And then came the moment when I realized that the darkness I was experiencing had come about because the light of grace was shining so brightly that it had temporarily blinded me.

It was then that I began to be free.

The Story after the Story

I HAVE JUST WRITTEN "I began to be free." And it was, truly, a beginning—but just a beginning. One of the people who read an earlier draft of this book scrawled the following comment across the page in which I wrote of my experience of releasing obsessions, jealousy, resentment, and anger:

> Okay, I realize that a five or six week retreat can be formative, but after eighteen years of a marriage I find it hard to believe that five weeks of a silent retreat totally transformed you. I trust you, but I find it a bit difficult to not think there is any residual anger, bitterness, hurt, or fear. Eighteen years is a long time.

He was right in pressing me in this way, and I'd be fooling myself if I tried to claim that my freedom from all of those things is complete. Like Jacob limping away from his long night of wrestling with the stranger by the ford of the Jabbok, there are times when I still limp, when I am still very aware of the scar tissue. There are reminders all around me, even in my new home. Pieces of furniture and art, dinnerware, photo albums and Christmas ornaments, books with warm inscriptions that still startle me: each of these is tied to a specific time or phase of a life no longer shared. The transformation, freedom, and healing in me are very real—but so are the memories, the sadness, and the lingering questions.

One of the things I had decided while I was at the Hermitage of the Annunciation was that I had to find myself a new place to call home. Within weeks of my return to Winnipeg I met with a realtor to begin going through the steps to ready the house for sale. I cleaned out shelves and closets, and made countless runs to the local thrift store to drop off boxes of goods I knew I would never use. Chipping away at the work a bit each day, the task of preparing for this move was not nearly so daunting as I had feared. And, strangely, one of the most gratifying tasks of all was the culling of my library.

In the third-floor study of the house we had 140 linear feet of bookshelves, and I knew I'd never have anything like that amount of space again, no matter where I landed. I began to go through those shelves, taking out each book and asking three simple questions:

1. Might I want to read or refer to this again?

2. Might I want to loan this out for someone else to read?

3. Does this one have particular significance, either because it was a gift or because it has had a real influence in the shaping of my thought and faith?

If I answered "yes" to any of the three questions, it was placed back on the shelf. Otherwise? Into a box it would go. That spring I hauled those boxes down to the main floor and set out the books on display on every flat surface available, just under 500 volumes in total. I sent out word that I was hosting a Saturday book sale, with everything available for just a dollar or two. As people arrived I would ask what they were interested in, and then take them to the area where those particular books were located. Time and again I would pluck up a volume and hand it to someone, suggesting that it might be one they would enjoy reading. Often as not I'd just tell them to take it, as the important thing to me was not the dollar or two but rather knowing that the book had landed in good hands.

By the end of that Saturday I'd moved close to 400 books, with the rest packed back into boxes and taken to a donation depot for our local Children's Hospital annual book sale. It was a good and satisfying day.

Even after this, though, I still had well over a thousand volumes in my library, and I was beginning to wonder if I'd ever find a place that had space for them. And then I noticed a property that seemed promising, not only because it had huge windows and high ceilings, but also because of what looked in the photographs to be built-in bookshelves. It was in an old retrofitted John Deere warehouse in Winnipeg's historic Exchange district. As I walked through the door with my realtor, I could see a wall of windows running right across the large living and dining room, facing out into the Western prairie sky. The windows stretched seven feet from bottom to top and sixteen feet across, framed by exposed brick on each side. Stepping further inside, I saw those bookcases, which ran from the hardwood floor right up to the high ceiling, filling the entire dining area wall. They were made of heavy timbers and stained a deep, rich brown, and I could see how beautifully they would house an awful lot of my library.

"I think this is it," I said.

And, as it turned out, this most certainly was the place that would become my home. As I sit now at my dining room table writing, I can look up at the wall of books, taking comfort in the familiarity of their spines. Like good friends, they share this space with me.

Along with my thoughts about moving to a new home, my journal entries from my weekend at the Hermitage of the Annunciation included the observation that I was feeling I would like to retire from parish ministry in the year that I turn sixty. I actually held on to that thought for a few months after my return to Winnipeg, but once I'd settled into my new home I began to think again. I'm sure that was partly on account of being finished the work of downsizing and moving, but it also had much to do with my church community's decision to permanently augment our staff team by adding a half-time ministry position, thus providing a bit more breathing space in my own pastoral work. The need or want to retire at sixty? Gone.

I hold close to my heart three very distinct signs from my five weeks pacing that cage in Halifax, and with these I will draw this book to a close.

Every time I walk in my door, I glance at the first sign, the icon I labored, prayed, and laughed over during those weeks in my cell. It is certainly not of a quality that would land it on an iconostasis in an Orthodox church—but it *is* far more an icon of Jesus than it is an image of a snowman or sun-bleached surfer dude. And it is *my* icon, such that when I gaze at it I can see written in the face of Christ all that I was working through over those five weeks. I'm reminded, too, that what I'd initially thought an impossible task came to fruition through long hours, prayerful support, and Ben's patient guidance. And isn't that a sort of icon, all of its own? When we're burdened, what might most be required is time for amendment of life—patience, prayer, and steadfast counsel and companionship. As I mentioned earlier, in the Communion liturgy of the Book of Common Prayer there is a set of scripture verses read after the confession, in what are known as "the comfortable words." Among them is Matthew 11.28: "Come unto me all that labour and are heavy laden, and I will refresh you." "Heavy laden" is exactly the state I was in when I entered my weeks of solitude.

I came into the Anglican Church in my early twenties, into a parish that used only the Book of Common Prayer, and I have never lost my love for that book. This love was rekindled during my time worshipping with the community of King's College Chapel—and here is the second sign I have held close since my retreat: since my return to Winnipeg I have incorporated the Psalter from the Book of Common Prayer into my practice of praying a daily office from the Church of England's liturgical resource, Common Worship: Morning and Evening Prayer. The juxtaposition of a contemporary daily office and the rich, poetic language of those psalms strikes me as a lovely and right expression of the breadth of the tradition in which I live.

Finally, the third sign: a little, rough-hewn stone cross, and the story that lies behind it. On Saturday afternoon at the student retreat, I noticed one of the Chapel community members scraping on a piece of soapstone with his pocketknife. I watched as the stone slowly took the shape of a stylized cross, finding it soothing and meditative simply to see his hands at work and to hear the gentle scraping of steel against stone. Later, on the way to the airport, Father Thorne reached into his jacket pocket, pulled out the cross and handed it to me. "Henk made this for you on the retreat," he said. "It is a gift that should live close to the altar." I was deeply moved by this young man's gesture, and thinking back now I still find it lovely that someone I had spoken to only in passing would offer such a gift. It "lives" most of the time on my bookshelf at home, but on Sundays I pack it carefully into my bag and take it with me to the church. As I begin to pray the Eucharistic prayer, I pick up that little stone cross and cradle it in the palm of my hand, right through to the breaking of the bread and the invitation to come forward for communion. Just three inches tall and two inches across, the rough little cross fits perfectly into my hand. It feels cool and solid against my skin, and that bit of extra weight in my palm somehow grounds me as I pray. I like its rough-hewn quality: it speaks more directly to me of the cross of Jesus than any finely wrought cross of silver or gold ever will.

Henk, along with Gary, Ben, and the other members of the Chapel community that year, this book is for you.

Under the mercy,
Jamie Howison

Photograph by Molly Robertson, used with permission

Bibliography

Archimandrite Sophrony. *St Silouan the Athonite.* Yonkers, NY: St. Vladimir's
Seminary Press, 1999.

The Book of Common Prayer. Toronto: Anglican Book Centre, 1962.

Carlin, Peter Ames. *Catch a Wave: The Rise, Fall, and Redemption of the Beach
Boys' Brian Wilson.* New York: Rodale, 2006.

Greene, Graham. *The Heart of the Matter.* 1948. New York: Penguin Books,
1982.

Lamott, Anne. *Traveling Mercies: Some Thoughts on Faith.* New York: Anchor,
2000.

L'Engle, Madeleine. *Two-Part Invention: The Story of a Marriage.* San Francisco:
Harper & Row, 1988.

Lindop, Grevel. *Charles Williams: The Third Inkling.* Oxford: Oxford University
Press, 2015.

The Monks of the Hermitage of the Annunciation. *Preparing for Confession: Life
in Christ—Healing and Ascetic Therapy.* New Germany, NS: Hermitage of
the Annunciation, 2014.

Norris, Kathleen. *Acedia & Me: A Marriage, Monks, and a Writer's Life.* New
York: Riverhead, 2008.

Saint-Exupéry, Antoine de. *The Little Prince.* Translated by Richard Howard.
San Diego: Harcourt, 2000.

Saint John's Abbey Prayer. Collegeville, MN: The Order of Saint Benedict Inc.,
1986.

Springsteen, Bruce. *Born to Run.* New York: Simon & Schuster, 2016.

Williams, Rowan. *The Dwelling of Light: Praying with Icons of Christ.* Toronto:
Novalis, 2003.

Zelensky, Elizabeth and Lela Gilbert. *Windows to Heaven: Introducing Icons to
Protestants and Catholics.* Grand Rapids, MI: Brazos, 2005.

CPSIA information can be obtained
at www.ICGtesting.com
Printed in the USA
BVHW040109310321
603675BV00002B/3